Manchester United:

The Official Season Guide 2014-15

Manchester United:

The Official Season Guide 2014-15

Steve Bartram
& Mark Froggatt

SIMON & SCHUSTER

London · New York · Sydney · Toronto · New Delhi

A CBS COMPANY

First published in Great Britain by Simon & Schuster UK Ltd, 2014
A CBS COMPANY

1 3 5 7 9 10 8 6 4 2

Simon & Schuster UK Ltd
1st Floor
222 Gray's Inn Road
London WC1X 8HB

www.simonandschuster.co.uk

Simon & Schuster Australia,Sydney
Simon & Schuster India,New Delhi

A CIP catalogue record for this book
is available from the British Library

ISBN: 978-1-47113-991-8

Typeset by M Rules
Printed and bound by CPI Group (UK) Ltd, Croydon, CR0 4YY

Contents

Acknowledgements   vi

Introduction   1

2013-14 Season Review   3

Meet the Manager: Louis van Gaal   49

Meet the Coaching Staff   55

Pre-season Tour 2014: United States   63

2014 – A Summer of Change   69

Leases of Life   73

The 2014-15 Squad Profiles   81

A Word from the Manager   229

Fixture List Season 2014-15   231

Acknowledgements

Sincere thanks go to Ian Marshall and his team at Simon & Schuster, particularly proof reader John Skermer and designer Nick Venables, for their sterling work in an especially short turnaround time.

At Manchester United, similar gratitude must go to Paul Thomas and James White once again for their customary but valuable role in the production process.

The extensive research for this book included excerpts from ManUtd.com, *United Review*, *Inside United* and England's national press outlets. All pictures used are provided by John and Matt Peters, on behalf of Manchester United.

Introduction

After spending over 26 years under the helmsmanship of one unparalleled genius of a manager, it was inevitable that Manchester United would require a time of transition to fully come to terms with the departure of Sir Alex Ferguson. The 2013-14 campaign was a tumultuous affair, with David Moyes leaving the club just ten months after replacing Ferguson. Ryan Giggs then called time on football's greatest career following the unexpected late plot twist of a stint as interim manager at his one and only club.

Joining the Welshman in departing the Old Trafford playing staff were fellow veterans Patrice Evra, Rio Ferdinand and Nemanja Vidic, while the growing sense of a new era was heightened by the appointment of the club's first foreign manager, Louis van Gaal, a highly decorated boss with a proven track record at various European giants. The Dutchman arrived fresh from guiding the Netherlands to an impressive third-place finish at the 2014 World Cup and immediately took the Reds on a successful pre-season tour of the United States. Having assessed his players' capabilities, van Gaal then oversaw extensive remodelling of the squad in the most remarkable summer of transfer business in the club's history.

Understandably, the wholesale changes made the early stages of the 2014-15 campaign less than straightforward, but an accomplished manager in charge of a top-class squad replete with devastating attacking talents represents cause for great excitement and enthusiasm at Old Trafford.

This book aims to introduce Manchester United in 2014-15. As well as looking back on the upheaval of 2013-14, we examine van Gaal and his new backroom staff, detail the club's pre-season tour and summer of substantial change, before providing in-depth profiles of the first-team players at the manager's disposal.

Such is the multi-cultural world of the modern United that squad members from the banks of the River Irwell mingle happily with those originating from the Amazon basin. Some have risen through our youth ranks to don the famous Red shirt each week, while others have undergone genuine hardships to join the world's biggest club in transfers from across the globe.

At a fascinating time in the club's history, this is your chance to learn more about the stories behind the players and the staff representing Manchester United in 2014-15. We hope you enjoy the book.

Steve Bartram and Mark Froggatt
September 2014, Manchester

2013-14 Season Review

The first season of the post-Sir Alex Ferguson era proved to be unforgettable on various levels, as a campaign which began on a high soon became an undulating, unpredictable ride . . .

August

Ironically, United's brave new era under David Moyes began with a nod to the past as fans congregated at Old Trafford to pay tribute to Rio Ferdinand for his 11 years of service. Although this testimonial was largely viewed as just another pre-season friendly, which was won 3-1 by La Liga outfit Sevilla, the occasion meant so much more to United's veteran defender: 'It's an honour to play for this club for so many years and I will continue to do so until they tell me to leave,' Rio explained, while addressing the crowd. 'Your support is much needed. We have a new manager now and everyone has got to get behind him.'

The occasion also saw Moyes contest his first home match as Reds boss, and the Glaswegian received a rousing ovation as he emerged from the tunnel at Old Trafford. While this was an important moment for Moyes, his eyes were fixed on the FA Community Shield and a chance to lift silverware in his first competitive match. As such, a strong XI was selected to face Wigan Athletic, who had just achieved the rare feat of winning the FA Cup while suffering relegation to the Championship. The Latics were duly dispatched thanks to Robin van Persie's double, and the Reds were off to a winning start.

'Moyes will surely feel a relieved man that his first high-profile engagement as United manager ended successfully,' wrote the *Daily Telegraph*'s Henry Winter. 'Defeat would have struck a discordant note amid the craved fanfares at the start of his reign.'

The feelgood factor was enhanced six days later via a 4-1 thrashing of Michael Laudrup's Swansea City at the Liberty Stadium, where van Persie and Danny Welbeck both struck twice to outweigh Wilfried Bony's riposte. Substitute Wayne Rooney also made an eye-catching cameo following a summer of speculation to notch two assists, providing another welcome boost for a manager who was struck by United's muted post-match celebrations.

'In the dressing room, it's quiet as they tell me it's what they do here – just move on to the next game,' Moyes explained. 'That's what I'm going to do as well.' Newly appointed player/coach Ryan Giggs, whose sumptuous pass assisted van Persie's opening goal, was also in bullish mood when quizzed on United's doubters. 'The players don't take any notice of where people expect us to finish,' the 39-year-old claimed. 'I got told last week that we were third favourites, but we know the quality we have got in the club.'

Chelsea were up next and, with the returning Jose Mourinho in charge, many had identified the Blues as strong contenders for the title. Moyes, therefore, faced his first real test under the glow of the Old Trafford floodlights. Encouragingly, United were by far the better team and controlled the game from start to finish. But like two pugilists afraid of a knockout blow, this stalemate did not live up to the hype. 'If this was to be the first instalment in a long fight for the prizes of English football, then Moyes v Mourinho Part I will not trouble the historians for too long,' observed Sam Wallace of the *Independent*.

Player of the Month – Robin van Persie

While much at United had changed over the summer, both on and off the pitch, van Persie's innate ability to score goals remained as potent as ever. The 2012-13 Player of the Year hit the ground running, netting braces against Wigan and Swansea before producing an industrial display during a nip-and-tuck stand-off with Chelsea at Old Trafford. As such, the Dutchman was somewhat unsurprisingly voted August's star man by Reds supporters around the world. 'It's always nice to win awards, especially when it's voted for by the fans who watch us every week, whether we're playing at Old Trafford or anywhere in the country,' Robin said. 'I'd like to thank all the fans who voted for me. I'm pleased to have scored four goals, but it's more important to me that the team has made a good start to the season.'

Game of the Month – United 2 Wigan Athletic 0, Community Shield

'This football club is used to winning trophies and we will do everything we can to make sure we win another,' explained a determined Moyes, prior to United's Community Shield encounter with FA Cup winners Wigan. While victory was expected under the Wembley arch, the Reds made light work of Owen Coyle's Latics and eased to a 2-0 win thanks to van Persie's brace. First-team debuts were also handed to 18-year-old Adnan Januzaj and new signing Wilfried

Zaha, who both continued their tour heroics with lively displays at the national stadium. After dedicating the victory to Sir Alex Ferguson, his predecessor, Moyes lifted silverware for the first time in his managerial career. As Chris Smalling explained, success can become infectious. 'Winning a trophy galvanises everyone and really helps you kick on. It's also great for Wilf and Adnan to experience the feeling – it really gets you in the zone and shows you what you're fighting for at this club.'

Goal of the Month – Robin van Persie (1st) vs Swansea City

All eyes were on the Liberty Stadium as the champions began their title defence against Swansea, and the Reds served up a spectacular opening to the new campaign – not least because of van Persie. The Dutchman needed just 34 minutes to break the deadlock with an acrobatic half-volley to set up what would become a hugely impressive 4-1 win. The unorthodox finish later earned praise from manager Moyes, who was delighted with his striker's effort. 'I think his foot was seven feet high in the air when he hit it. It was great athleticism and a good pass by Ryan Giggs that got us in.' Van Persie went on to score another eye-catching effort, lashing into the top corner from range, before exiting with just minutes left to play. As the *Guardian*'s Danny Taylor noted: 'Even the Swansea fans joined in the applause when he was substituted and, on this evidence, the Dutchman looks set for another wonderful season.'

September

After taking a four-point haul from their two opening Premier League fixtures, United could reflect on a respectable start to the new campaign. That was important for David Moyes's side, as September lined the well-trodden path with imposing obstacles – namely league trips to Anfield and the Etihad Stadium, as well as a taxing Capital One Cup tie at home to Liverpool and the commencement of Moyes's first tilt at the Champions League proper.

The month opened with a Sunday sortie across the East Lancashire Road, to meet a Liverpool side which had started brightly in its second season under Brendan Rodgers. An early Daniel Sturridge header proved sufficient to inflict United's first defeat of the season after a dour game of few chances, but Nemanja Vidic was far from downbeat afterwards. 'From every game you can take positives and negatives, even from this one,' said the skipper. 'I think in both games against Liverpool and Chelsea we were really solid, we didn't give our opponents anything. I don't remember having such an easy game at the back. We had so many crosses and they didn't look very dangerous. Not scoring is not like us, but it is still the beginning of the season and we have so many games to play, some tough games. I would not say we are worried but we have to improve some areas.'

Moyes sought to hasten that process with the deadline-day capture of Marouane Fellaini, renewing a relationship which began when the Scot signed the Belgian for Everton five years earlier. The towering midfielder was the Reds' sole recruit after a summer of intense speculation, but just as important was the refusal to countenance Chelsea's repeated enquiries for Wayne Rooney. The England striker had missed the trip to Anfield after suffering a deep gash on his forehead in training, and he was forced to don protective headgear in order to make his return against Palace the following weekend.

As the Reds registered a first home win of the league season against Crystal Palace, Rooney notched his opening goal of the campaign, a crisp free-kick to embellish Robin van Persie's opener from the penalty spot, to the delight of his manager. 'We wanted to try to get Wayne through ninety minutes,' explained Moyes. 'It was a difficult decision [to play him], but we were trying to see him in training with the headband on and he felt okay with it. He felt he could wear it so we thought we'd try and get him out.

'I felt he tired a little bit in the second half, but I wanted to keep him on, get some minutes under his belt, and get him ready for the coming weeks and months. Goalscorers want to score, and Robin and Wayne got goals today. That's what we want.'

Merely appearing in a Red shirt provided a source of satisfaction for Fellaini, who debuted midway through the second half and was quick to offer his thanks for a warm welcome at Old Trafford. 'It was a fantastic debut and we won, which was most important,' he said. 'I was both nervous and excited. I would like to say thank you to the supporters, it was good for me. Every time I will give my maximum for the club and for my team-mates. United want to win every game and we won today so it was good for our confidence ahead of the next game – because the next game is a big game, it is a Champions League game. So this is good for the confidence.'

There was plenty of swagger about United as Bayer Leverkusen arrived in Manchester to begin an unfamiliar Champions League group also comprising Real Sociedad and Shakhtar Donetsk. Rooney opened the scoring and, though Simon Rolfes briefly levelled for the visitors, second-half efforts from van Persie, Rooney again and Antonio Valencia negated Omer Toprak's late consolation strike. For United's No.10, the evening carried special significance as his brace made him only the fourth player to reach the 200-goal milestone for the club.

'It's gone very quick and I am very pleased to have scored two hundred goals for a club like Manchester United,' said the striker. 'It's a great honour for me. Hopefully there will be more to come. I'm concentrating on my football as I have done all summer. I've got my head down and I've worked really hard. I got myself ready for the season and I'm delighted with the way I have come back. I'm delighted to be back playing and scoring goals.'

Even the eye-catching resurgence of Rooney would prove insufficient to help United in the first Manchester derby of the season, however. Shorn of the injured van Persie, Moyes's men were outclassed in embarrassing fashion and found themselves four goals down by the 50th minute at the Etihad Stadium. The situation prompted an improved performance and a late rally, but only Rooney's free-kick provided tangible reward on a chastening afternoon across the city.

'It's not nice to lose to City by four goals to one,' said United's goalscorer. 'To lose by any score is bad, so we're all really disappointed. The way we conceded the goals – one just before half time and two straight after – is not good enough. We know we have to improve on that, to stop giving these sloppy goals away and capitalise on some of our good play, which just came too late in the game. We knew at four-nil that we obviously weren't getting back into the game, but we had to keep fighting and pressing, trying to make a game of it to show the fans, and ourselves, the pride we have as footballers as it's never nice to lose.'

Pride suitably stung, it was imperative that United made a swift statement of intent, and the Capital One Cup visit of Liverpool provided an ideal opening just three days later. The game unfolded into an infinitely more entertaining spectacle than the drab fare served up at Anfield earlier in the month, and an open, end-to-end encounter was settled moments after half time by Chicharito's adroit finish.

'I think sometimes in the box it's your movement so you can lose big defenders and markers,' explained Moyes. 'I think Chicha did that and he's done great – his movement in the box is terrific. It's real centre-forward movement. He's great in the box and he gets his goals that way. A lot of credit must go to him for the way he finished it as well. It's okay losing his marker, but the way he adjusted his body to get the finish away means it was a really good goal from our point of view at a good time in the game.'

But the rollercoaster theme of September continued into its final game. The visit of West Bromwich Albion had been framed as the light at the end of the tunnel, following a flurry of meetings with established title contenders, but instead United were alarmingly outplayed at Old Trafford. Rooney once again struck from a free-kick to cancel out Morgan Amalfitano's solo strike, but the visitors scored again through Saido Berahino to deservedly register their first win at United since 1978.

'It was a poor result and a poor performance – we never really got going,' conceded Moyes. 'We lacked an intensity and spark to our game, and in the end they deserved the win, I can't argue with that. I thought for all our possession we didn't create a lot of opportunities. And when we did, we didn't take them. We had plenty of forward players out there, but we're just not opening teams up. I'm concerned after today, but there are a lot of games to go and we'll try to put it right.'

Player of the Month – Wayne Rooney

With the transfer window shut, the Reds' No.10 was able to put a summer of speculation behind him and he served a timely, sustained reminder of his talents over the course of September. Rooney began the month on the sidelines after suffering a deep gash on his forehead in a training session, but returned with the clinching goal as Moyes registered his first home win at the expense of Crystal Palace. That free-kick against the Eagles commenced a run of five goals in as many games throughout the month, with set-pieces scored in defeats to Manchester City and West Brom, while a clinical brace against Bayer Leverkusen marked a winning start to the Reds' Champions League campaign. 'I was really impressed with the condition Wayne was in and the work he did in pre-season,' explained Moyes, 'and he is getting the fruits of that. He's worked hard and is showing everyone exactly what he can do.'

Game of the Month – United 4 Bayer Leverkusen 2, Champions League

The *Daily Telegraph*'s Henry Winter declared an entertaining, goal-laden opening to the Reds' Champions League tilt as: 'A victory for Moyes in many senses; not only was this win over Leverkusen a largely convincing start to his first European campaign at United but his astute handling of the Rooney saga has been rewarded.' Rooney was the star turn, netting the game's opener from close range despite three credible claims for a disallowance from Leverkusen. The striker then became only the fourth player to score 200 goals for the club by converting United's third, and rounded off the evening with an assist for Valencia. Simon Rolfes had briefly levelled for the Bundesliga visitors before van Persie volleyed home, and a late consolation from Omer Toprak couldn't take the gloss off an evening of promise at Old Trafford.

Goal of the Month – Wayne Rooney vs Manchester City

It counted for precious little on the day, but there was an element of justice in the manner of Rooney's late consolation strike at the Etihad Stadium. The striker was United's outstanding performer as Manuel Pellegrini's side ran riot in the September sunshine, prompting Moyes to suggest: 'I thought Wayne was arguably the best player on the pitch. He certainly didn't deserve to play on the losing team.' Though that outcome had long since been assured, with City 4-0 up by the 50-minute mark, Rooney salvaged a modicum of pride with a sublime free-kick three minutes from time, bending his effort beautifully into Joe Hart's top corner from 25 yards. 'It's nice to score, but it means nothing,' the striker could only shrug. 'It was too little, too late.'

October

Start slowly and finish strongly; a United hallmark that applied itself to the month of October, when two draws and four wins were gleaned from six matches in all competitions. It began with a Champions League trek to Ukraine and Shakhtar Donetsk, who pilfered a 1-1 draw thanks to Taison's 76th-minute strike after Danny Welbeck had opened the scoring in the first half. While an impressive victory was unfortunately let slip at the Donbass Arena, the Longsight lad wasn't too disappointed after the final whistle. 'Not many teams come here and win,' Welbeck told reporters. 'We would have liked to have got all three points, but it just wasn't to be.'

Just three days later, another long journey to the North-East was completed for a Premier League showdown with Sunderland, under the caretaker charge of Kevin Ball. A sluggish start allowed Craig Gardner to rifle the Black Cats into a deserved half-time lead and United could have been in deeper trouble had David De Gea not saved magnificently from Emanuele Giaccherini's header. Then, with the game on a knife-edge, 18-year-old Adnan Januzaj celebrated his first league start with a crisply taken double strike that introduced him to the world. 'Exuding class and confidence in a manner that few of his team-mates were able to manage, the fresh-faced player signed two years ago from Anderlecht looks very much like the answer to most of Moyes's immediate problems,' wrote the *Guardian*'s Paul Wilson.

A home game with Southampton followed, and Januzaj – fresh from signing a five-year contract – produced another moment of brilliance to assist Robin van Persie's opener midway through the first half. Alas, another afternoon of frustration followed as Saints captain Adam Lallana restored parity in the 89th minute, leaving Moyes's men eight points behind leaders Arsenal after as many games. Thankfully, a European tie under the Old Trafford floodlights required instant focus and the Reds moved closer to the knockout stages with a narrow 1-0 win over Real Sociedad, a triumph ensured by Inigo Martinez's own goal – which owed much to superb work by Wayne Rooney. 'It was important we won after Saturday's result,' the England international concluded. 'We defended well and we created a lot of chances. On another day we'd have won more comfortably.'

Mark Hughes's Stoke City were next up at the Theatre of Dreams and deservedly led at half time through Peter Crouch and Marko Arnautovic, whose goals bookended van Persie's close-range finish. Thankfully, spurred on by a raucous crowd, the Reds turned it around with two late headers from Rooney and Javier Hernandez. Moyes hoped it was the 'first of many comebacks', but Patrice Evra, always a rousing motivational talker, confessed concern about United's newfound inability to build momentum. 'We can't win one game, draw the next or lose the next one. We want to win two games in a row, three games in a row, but I say: "When are we going to start to win ten matches in a row?" That's when we can say Manchester United are back in business.'

Having tackled three outings in a week, Moyes rang the changes for a Capital One Cup fourth-round tie with Norwich City in which Wilfried Zaha made his first appearance since the Community Shield win over Wigan. The manager's gamble paid off and United bagged a comfortable 4-0 win thanks to goals from Hernandez (2), Phil Jones and Fabio da Silva. Assistant manager Steve Round, taking up post-match media duties for the first time, was elated with the reshuffled team's performance, stressing: 'We made nine changes and it was still a really strong side. This bodes well for the future.'

Player of the Month – Adnan Januzaj

Talk of a teenage sensation oozing style and grace had been building for several months, but by the end of October, after netting a headline-stealing brace at Sunderland, the secret of Adnan Januzaj was finally out. He became a *bona fide* star overnight and, unsurprisingly, a terrace idol among Reds supporters. The Belgian's heroics at the Stadium of Light were swiftly followed by another Man-of-the-Match display against Southampton, before ink was significantly scribbled across a new five-year contract. Upon signing that deal, the then 18-year-old was acutely aware that this was just the start of his remarkable tale. 'This season has been great for me – going on the pre-season tour, making my debut in the Community Shield win at Wembley and then breaking into the team at Sunderland – it's like a dream,' he said. 'I want to work hard now and establish myself as a Manchester United player.'

Game of the Month – Sunderland 1 United 2, Premier League

United travelled to Sunderland on the back of harrowing Premier League defeats to Manchester City and West Brom, rendering this Saturday tea-time kick-off a must-win for Moyes's men. A sluggish start saw the Black Cats take a lead through Craig Gardner, however, before the Reds eventually sparked into life and equalised thanks to Januzaj's elegant right-footer that sailed past goalkeeper Keiren Westwood. The baby-faced Belgian would save his best for last, though, as an audacious volley from John O'Shea's failed clearance flew into the bottom corner, illuminating his full debut. De Gea made a key contribution to deny Giaccherini with a save that goalkeeping legend Peter Schmeichel later described as 'one of the best seen in the Premier League', but even the Spaniard had to cede centre stage to Januzaj. 'We have a lot to thank him for,' admitted Michael Carrick. 'Those were two great finishes. He's got a great attitude and lots of ability. He looks a proper player.'

Goal of the Month – Adnan Januzaj (2nd) vs Sunderland

Rooney's arced header against Stoke City deserved applause, as well as Jones's technically astute volley in the League Cup, but neither goal could live up to the style and verve of Januzaj's wonderful winner against the Black Cats. 'This was one of the best days of my life, scoring two goals on my debut,' Adnan later explained. 'The second one was harder because it came to me on the edge of the box and it was hard to execute. I just shot and hoped the ball was going in! I was happy that day and will always have special memories of it.' Even Rooney, no stranger to spectacular strikes, was impressed, conceding: 'To volley a ball like that and guide it into a corner takes a lot of ability and technique. It was also a vital goal for us.'

November

Unbeaten throughout October after a dreadful September, United knew that November would be a key month in reeling in Premier League pacesetters Arsenal and making progress in the cup competitions.

The month's action began in suitably spritely fashion, with Fulham comfortably overcome in double-quick time at Craven Cottage as the attacking quartet of Antonio Valencia, Wayne Rooney, Adnan Januzaj and Robin van Persie tore the Cottagers to pieces. Valencia's opener was followed by a goal apiece from van Persie and Rooney inside the first 22 minutes, rendering the rest of the game a formality and Alex Kacaniklic's second-half strike of inconsequence.

'It was good, especially the opening twenty minutes, as we got off to a blistering start and the boys put us in a great position,' enthused David Moyes. 'We looked like we were ready to really rip them apart at times. We scored three and created a number of other moves that could have ended up in goals, so I've got to say I was really pleased with that part of the game. I thought there were signs today that Wayne and Robin were really clicking. They created chances for one another. Anyone who has been a centre-forward, you're always looking for your partner to do well and they both did that today, they worked really well together, especially in the early part of the game.'

There would be no such rip-roaring action when the Reds travelled to Real Sociedad three days later, as a second successive Champions League away tie ended in a stalemate. Van Persie's uncharacteristic wastefulness from the penalty spot spurned the chance to take all three points, but wily veteran Ryan Giggs was far from distraught to have reached eight points with two group games remaining.

'We had two or three great chances and probably should have won the game,' said the player-coach. 'We are probably happy with the performance but disappointed that we didn't get the three points, but if you get a point away from home and win your home games then you usually go through and we are on track to do that at the moment, so hopefully we can finish the job off. We have got two tough games left to play but we are up for the task. We have played both Shakhtar and Leverkusen, we know what they are all about and we are confident of going through.'

While United were leading from the front in Group A, the Premier League table was far grimmer reading for Moyes's men. With eight wins from ten games, Arsenal were already threatening to leave the reigning champions for dust, and an away victory when the sides met at Old Trafford would have resulted in an 11-point gap after as many games. Mindful of the game's must-win status, United turned in a display of graft and guile to deservedly take the spoils through van Persie's first-half header.

'We could have been eleven points behind, so now we're in a good position,' said the match-winner. 'It was a big win, a real six-pointer. We are right in the mix, which is what we wanted. We realised that it was a must-win game. I always think positively, and I'm thankful that we did that today. I don't think it is enough for a couple of individuals to play well; I think you need to be strong as a team, that's what we did today. The fans were incredible; they really lifted us and were the twelfth man.'

Though the home support at Old Trafford had plenty to shout about after a welcome show of authority, an untimely international break made for a fortnight's wait until the Reds' next outing, which had a far less satisfactory outcome. Rooney and Patrice Evra struck either side of ex-Red Fraizer Campbell to put the champions ahead at promoted Cardiff City, but a sloppy late concession to Kim Bo-Kyung substantially lessened the Reds' momentum.

Putting a brave face on the setback, veteran defender Rio Ferdinand proffered: 'We're unhappy we didn't close the game out but, looking back at the end of the season, we may say this was a point gained rather than two lost. The equaliser was the last free-kick of the game and a silly one to give away – we didn't defend it as well as we should have. It's happened a couple of times this season and we have to put it right. But nothing's given out now so it doesn't matter what the table looks like, as long as we're within touching distance. We'll keep looking to pick up points, build momentum and push our way up the table.'

While time remained for United to play the long game in the title race, qualification for the knockout stages of the Champions League would be made or broken by two remaining group games: a tricky-looking trip to Bayer Leverkusen preceding a group finale against seasoned dark horses Shakhtar Donetsk. Yet, for all the potential pitfalls in store, Moyes's men ensured qualification with a game to spare with an astonishing 5-0 win in Germany, brought about by Valencia and an Emir Spahic own-goal before the break, and second-half goals from Jonny Evans, Chris Smalling and Nani.

'I think we were due a performance like that,' grinned Smalling, having opened his account for the season. 'For a large part of previous games, we have dominated but never really killed off a team. Defensively, we were sound and, going forward, we looked a threat as Shinji Kagawa, Antonio Valencia and Nani wreaked havoc. We just said: "Go out and run at them" to our attacking players and they did that. For us to really demolish Bayer was pleasing. Nobody is really tired in the dressing room, the enthusiasm is really up.'

Through with a match to spare in Europe, having beaten the Premier League leaders and having amassed a run of 11 games without defeat, there was plenty of cause for optimism as 2013 moved into its final month.

Player of the Month – Wayne Rooney

United found the net 11 times in November, and Rooney was involved in nine of them including two goals – at Fulham and Cardiff City – and five direct assists. Four of the latter came in one game as Rooney played a key role in the obliteration of Leverkusen, and the Reds' No.10 was happy to contribute in any way possible. 'I've always worked on [getting assists],' he said. 'Thankfully the lads are getting on the end of the deliveries now! It's great when you put a good ball into the box and someone gets on the end of it to score. And we also aim to keep clean sheets. That means the forwards have to come back and help out from set-pieces.' Having tracked back with his customary gusto as well as providing goals galore, the omnipresent striker was a shoo-in as November's star man.

Game of the Month5 – Bayer Leverkusen 0 United 5, Champions League

No contest. In the ruthless obliteration of Sami Hyypia's Bayer Leverkusen, United posted their biggest away victory in European competition since 1957's 6-0 trouncing of Shamrock Rovers. Moyes's side were aware that three points would seal qualification to the knock-out stages with a game to spare, but none could have foreseen the emphatic nature in which they would be secured: scoring five goals without reply and dominating from start to finish. 'I've been hoping to get this type of performance more often, I've not had it as often as I would have liked,' admitted Moyes. 'Leverkusen are doing so well in the Bundesliga at the moment, second only to Bayern Munich, so that puts our result and performance into perspective. It was an all-round great performance, coming away from home and scoring five goals somewhere that's renowned as being a difficult place to come.'

Goal of the Month – Nani vs Bayer Leverkusen

Despite the boon of signing a new, long-term contract, Nani's season had been decimated by injury, reducing him to just five starts prior to late November's Champions League trip to Leverkusen. His first goal of the campaign was worth the wait. A curling, lofted pass from Giggs allowed the Portuguese to outpace the home defenders and race onto the ball just inside the area, where his sublime chest control took him past goalkeeper Bernd Leno. All that remained was to flick home an audacious finish which belied the unforgiving angle of its execution. 'It was a great goal and I'm happy,' enthused the goalscorer. 'Scoring five goals away from home is not easy against a German team. We tried to exploit the counter-attack, had opportunities and took them and that's why we scored five goals.' With the best, fittingly, saved until last.

December

At a time of traditional indulgence for fans, the festive excess included a considerable nine fixtures for United in the busiest month of the season. The glut of games began with a testing trip to Tottenham, who came into the game with manager Andre Villas-Boas under growing pressure following a 6-0 mauling at the hands of Manchester City. In contrast, the Reds were unbeaten in 11 and managed to extend that run thanks to Wayne Rooney's brace, which earned a dramatic 2-2 draw after goals from Kyle Walker and Sandro had twice put Spurs in front. 'We're on a good run at the minute,' Rooney observed at the final whistle. 'But we need to turn some of these draws into wins.'

Unfortunately, the Reds did exactly the opposite and went on to suffer two devastating 1-0 home defeats to Everton and Newcastle in just four days, halting all of the positive momentum gained through-out October and November. Those losses also meant that David Moyes's men had dropped 13 points out of 24 at Old Trafford, a record almost unheard of in the modern era. With a worrying pattern emerging, the *Guardian*'s Paul Wilson wrote: 'This is not the first time Manchester United have lost Premier League games back to back without scoring; it did happen under Sir Alex Ferguson, but the worry for David Moyes is that his side have lost a third of their league games to date and Old Trafford has lost almost all of its capacity to intimidate.'

An opportunity to bounce back soon arrived with the Champions League Group A finale against Shakhtar Donetsk, and the Reds' domestic woes were shelved as a tight 1-0 victory secured top spot with a haul of 14 points from a possible 18 – the club's best haul since 2007-08. Phil Jones scored the only goal with a clinical second-half volley to cap a powerful display in midfield. Afterwards, the match-winner was adamant that his team-mates had to improve domestically. 'Hopefully we can now start picking up some points in the league,' he explained. 'It starts on Sunday against Aston Villa. They're a tricky team but we have to go there and get three points.'

The bad news from the victory over Ukraine's finest was an injury to talismanic striker Robin van Persie, who was immediately ruled out for up to a month with a groin strain. Thankfully, United's ranks were boosted by the return of Darren Fletcher following his long battle with the bowel condition ulcerative colitis. The popular Scot made a much-welcomed cameo as a substitute during a 3-0 win at Villa Park, where two goals from Danny Welbeck and a third from Tom Cleverley clinched a promising victory over an under-par opposition. Fletcher's return provided an overwhelming positive, however, and the midfielder was determined to make up for lost time. 'This is it, I'm back for good,' he declared. 'This is hopefully the game which means I'm back now. I seem to have come through the setbacks and health issues and I'm thankful for that. It's onwards and upwards now.'

With Christmas approaching, the fixtures were stacking up and, just three days later, United were back in action for a Capital One Cup quarter-final against Stoke City. While the Britannia Stadium is renowned for eschewing warm welcomes, a faintly ludicrous spectacle unfolded as strong winds and heavy hailstones wreaked havoc to force a ten-minute first-half stoppage. Once play had resumed, two stunning strikes from Ashley Young and Patrice Evra earned a gutsy 2-0 win and booked a semi-final showdown with Sunderland. But it was far from easy, as Welbeck later acknowledged. 'At one point, when I had the ball, I was actually running blind – I couldn't see where I was going,' the striker told reporters. 'I knew a defender was around me but I didn't know how close he was. The conditions were definitely the worst I've ever played in.'

The final home match of 2013 saw the Reds secure a comfortable 3-1 win over Sam Allardyce's relegation-threatened West Ham, with Welbeck notching his first goal at Old Trafford in over 14 months before Adnan Januzaj grabbed his maiden strike in M16. Young then added the decisive third – and his second in as many matches – before Carlton Cole notched a late consolation for the Hammers. Speaking afterwards, 28-year-old winger Young was clearly delighted with his improved form in front of goal. 'Before midweek, I hadn't scored in eighteen or nineteen months and to get two in a week is fantastic. It's like when buses come along! It was vitally important to win now that we are going into this busy Christmas and New Year period.'

A Boxing Day trip to Hull City required United to climb off the canvas and come from two goals down following early concessions to former Reds defender James Chester and David Meyler during a breathless opener. Chris Smalling then nodded home in the 19th minute before Rooney restored parity with a deliciously swerved volley from 25 yards, beating helpless goalkeeper Allan McGregor. Chester's second – an unfortunate own goal midway through the second half – clinched a remarkable away victory, though the sight of Antonio Valencia being sent off for a second yellow card did not please Moyes. Steve Bruce was also disappointed by his side's collapse, but retained his sense of humour when asked for his next move: 'Go home, kick the cat, have a glass of red.'

United's ninth and final match of December warranted a long trip to Norwich City and Carrow Road, where the taxing festive schedule eventually took its toll on a match that was largely controlled by the Canaries. The Reds were struggling and, dismayed by his team's performance, Moyes intervened by introducing Welbeck for Ryan Giggs. His decision paid dividends as the substitute blocked Ryan Bennett's clearance before executing a clinical finish past John Ruddy to seal a vital 1-0 win that left United in sixth place and seven points shy of leaders Arsenal. When asked for his mid-season report after the final whistle, the manager cast his eye towards a much-improved second half. 'If you're only assessing the Premier League, you'd like it to be better. But if you're assessing the cup games and all that as well, I think we've done okay. We'd like the league position to be better but we'll keep trying to achieve that.'

Player of the Month – Wayne Rooney

Six appearances, four assists and three goals were the numbers attached to Rooney's name by the end of the busy festive schedule, taking him to 23 outings and 11 strikes for the first half of what was becoming a testing season. As manager Moyes told reporters just before Christmas, United's No.10 was becoming an increasingly influential figure in the dressing room. 'Wayne has turned himself into a real team player. The assists for the team, the goals and his all-round contribution has been fantastic,' the boss enthused. 'He looks as if he is beginning to take ownership himself. He is starting to say: "Look, come on, we need to play better. We need to make sure we are doing much more than we are doing."'

Game of the Month – Hull City 2 United 3, Premier League

The Reds' comeback win at Hull became a slugfest that was entirely appropriate for the much-loved Boxing Day programme, sending Reds supporters back across the Humber Bridge with plenty of festive cheer. It had everything: from the Reds arriving at the stadium late due to traffic, a delay that forced Moyes to phone in his team sheet, to Valencia's 90th-minute dismissal for time-wasting. Most importantly, there were five goals as well, including one absolute corker from Rooney. 'To determine whether United can genuinely challenge for the title requires more than a dramatic victory at Hull, but the club trailed Newcastle by ten points on Christmas Day 1995 and won the title by four points,' wrote the *Daily Telegraph*'s Mark Ogden. 'Eighteen years on, the field is more competitive, but if

United continue to show the same fighting spirit when Robin van Persie and Nemanja Vidic return to action, who knows how the second half of the campaign will unfold.'

Goal of the Month – Wayne Rooney vs Hull City

Januzaj's well-crafted finish against West Ham will live long in the memory, partly because it was the young Belgian's first at Old Trafford, but only one goal deserved this accolade in December. 'The ball came in to me so I tried to chest it and play Danny Welbeck in but I mis-hit it a little bit,' explained Rooney, dissecting his stunning volley in the 3-2 comeback win at the KC Stadium. 'Danny readjusted his body and somehow got it back to me. I took it on the knee, let it bounce and then volleyed it. Thankfully it went in! I tried to curl the ball outside the post and then bring it back in. Thankfully, that's exactly what happened and it was a nice goal.' Incidentally, the last time Rooney faced Hull he scored all the goals in a 4-0 home win, but on this occasion, he registered his 150th Premier League goal for the club with one of his very best.

January

Having ended 2013 on the up with a run of four straight Premier League wins, allied to the commencement of the FA Cup and the resumption of the Capital One Cup at the semi-final stage, United had cause for substantial optimism as the New Year began. Instead, the Reds would suffer a nightmarish opening to 2014 to set the tone for a miserable second half of the campaign.

A month on from drawing 2-2 at White Hart Lane, the Reds hosted a Tottenham side newly managed by Tim Sherwood, who had replaced Andre Villas-Boas shortly before Christmas. Having won at

Old Trafford for the first time in 23 years in 2012-13, Spurs repeated the feat with breakaway goals from Emmanuel Adebayor and Christian Eriksen, outweighing Danny Welbeck's neat consolation strike for the hosts.

'We got done on the counter-attack for a couple of goals and made a couple of mistakes,' lamented David Moyes, 'but I thought the team played very well. The players played very well. Their effort was terrific to try and get back into the game after being two-nil down. I actually thought when we got the goal back that we'd go on and win the game, never mind draw it; with the amount of chances we had, we really should have done so.'

In such a packed schedule, the Reds didn't have to wait long for an opportunity to bounce back. Four days on came the FA Cup third-round visit of Swansea City, who had never before won at Old Trafford. That looked like remaining the case as the game drifted towards a 1-1 draw, after Chicharito had cancelled out Wayne Routledge's early opener, only for the dismissal of Fabio to hand the impetus to the visitors, who dumped United out of the competition through Wilfried Bony's injury-time header.

'It's a massive blow, let's not kid ourselves: this is a bad result,' admitted Darren Fletcher. 'There are a lot of angry, hurt players and we feel like we've let the manager and the fans down. We should have gone on and finished the game off, or definitely taken the lead. We never managed to do that and the red card gave them a great boost in the last ten minutes, and they went on to get the winning goal. We've got to recover quickly and lift ourselves now, because we've got a League Cup semi-final [at Sunderland] coming up. If you can't lift yourself for that then it's no good.'

But there would be no immediate recovery for the Reds, who endured another dark night at the Stadium of Light. The first own-goal of Ryan Giggs's career gave Sunderland a first-half lead and, although Nemanja Vidic powered in a header to equalise, the hosts ensured themselves a lead to take into the second leg when Fabio Borini converted a controversial penalty, awarded for Tom Cleverley's perceived trip on Adam Johnson.

'We did not have that little bit of luck,' stressed Giggs. 'It just did not go for us. We'll keep plugging away and we'll look forward to the second leg. We are still in it, and we look forward to it at Old Trafford. The only chances they really had were set-pieces. It was just one of those nights. I have said over the years that the defeats and losses generate a bigger feeling than winning things. It sticks with you a lot longer. You have to react and you have to try to do something about it. There are a lot of players who have come into the club who have only known winning. It is a test of character, but I am fully confident we will come through it and we will be okay.'

Fresh from their maiden win at Old Trafford and eager to inflict a fourth straight defeat on Moyes's men, Swansea returned to Manchester but were comfortably dealt with as the Reds turned in a much-improved display and returned to winning ways through close-range efforts from Antonio Valencia and Welbeck.

Unfortunately, the chances of rebuilding some much-needed momentum were not helped by the daunting nature of the next game: a trip to face Chelsea at Stamford Bridge. Though the Blues were hardly at their fluid best, their unbeaten home Premier League record under Jose Mourinho underlined the size of the task at hand. From the moment Samuel Eto'o cracked home a deflected opening goal after 17 minutes, United always looked to be up against it, and further concessions either side of the interval rendered Chicharito's late consolation goal futile.

'The end of the first half killed us,' Michael Carrick opined. 'To find ourselves two-nil down was a blow. Then we said at half time that if we got the next goal, we'd be right in the game, but it was an uphill task when the third one went in. Both those goals came at bad times. We need to create more ourselves. The fans have been unbelievable over the last month or so and we have a lot to thank them for. If we all stick together, I'm sure it'll turn soon. We'll keep fighting – that's what we do. Our next game [the semi-final decider against Sunderland] is another huge game for us, an opportunity to get to a final. We'll get over this, dust ourselves down and get ready for it.'

Few could have prepared for what would unfold when Gus Poyet's side visited Old Trafford, however. Jonny Evans nudged in a close-range finish to draw the tie level, but a low-key display from both sides allowed the game to drift to a painfully dull extra-time session which only sparked into life in its final minute. Firstly, in the 119th minute, David De Gea allowed Phil Bardsley's speculative effort to creep in, only for Chicharito to turn in a last-gasp finish which took the game to penalties. In one of the poorest shootouts on record, Sunderland won 2-1 as only three of the ten penalty-takers managed to convert their kicks.

A stunned Moyes made no excuses, admitting: 'I've got no complaints. I just don't think we had a level of performance that merited winning the game more comfortably, and that's what I was looking for. If we'd gone through I'd have been disappointed in the performance, but obviously I'm doubly disappointed because we didn't get through. With a minute to go, we were in the final. Then we had a chance when it went to penalties, but we were terrible at penalty kicks. We didn't play well enough tonight and Sunderland came here and deservedly got themselves into the final.'

A timely boon was provided, however, before the transfer window closed, as Spanish international Juan Mata was enlisted from Chelsea for a club record £37.1 million fee. 'I like the pressure,' he grinned. 'I think it's good to try and improve when you have pressure – people are expecting big things from me and I'm looking forward to trying to do that and make all these amazing fans happy.'

A hand in both United goals on his debut – a 2-0 win over Ole Gunnar Solskjaer's Cardiff, secured through goals by Robin van

Persie and Ashley Young – constituted an impressive start for Mata, who afterwards beamed: 'It was a very special day for me. My first game – my debut – and a victory. It was perfect. The most important thing was we won and I felt comfortable with my team-mates.'

The Spaniard's arrival represented cause for buoyancy which had been rocked by an otherwise harrowing month. With less than four months of the season to go, United had no margin for error remaining if the title or Champions League qualification were to remain viable targets.

Player of the Month – Adnan Januzaj

At a time when there was difficulty in looking beyond grim immediacy, the excellence of Januzaj provided a cause for long-term optimism. A year earlier, the Belgian had been turning out for Paul McGuinness's Under-18s, but showed no fear when fast-tracked up to senior duties, and earned his manager's trust sufficiently to appear in every January game, starting five and entering two. Adnan began the month with a sublime assist for Welbeck against Spurs and particularly caught the eye against Sunderland in the Capital One Cup and Swansea in the Premier League. He split his time between a central role and his customary wing berth in the latter, and Moyes later explained: 'Adnan can play in all the positions – any one of the front roles. He's a top player. We've been saying it for a long time and he's at the right club.'

Game of the Month – United 2 Swansea City 0, Premier League

Slim pickings for this honour. Of United's seven January games – factoring in Sunderland's defeat but ensuing penalty shootout win – only Swansea and Cardiff were overcome. The former came after a run of three successive harrowing defeats, prompting an outpouring of emotion and wild scenes of celebration as Michael Laudrup's side were beaten. A dimly lit first period had been sporadically enlightened by the twinkling talent of Januzaj, and the Belgian youngster further illuminated the game after the break with a superb display down the left flank. The 18-year-old was heavily involved in the decisive goals, supplying crosses which were ultimately turned home by Valencia and Welbeck to provide David Moyes with some timely cheer and prevent the Reds from losing four straight games for the first time since 1961.

Goal of the Month – Ashley Young vs Cardiff City

In a month when jaws remained dropped for the most part, the only positives to have United fans agog were the signature of Mata and Young's blockbusting effort against Cardiff City. With the Reds leading Solskjaer's side by a single van Persie goal, Young picked up the ball on the left flank, meandered inside and arrowed a thunderous 25-yard drive into David Marshall's far corner. 'It ranks up there with my best,' said the winger. 'As soon as I struck it, I thought it had a good chance of going in and I think I was celebrating before it hit the back of the net.'

February

After a wretched January had ended on the up with the capture of Juan Mata and the defeat of Cardiff City, United supporters travelled to Stoke City encouraged by the prospect of seeing Wayne Rooney, Robin van Persie and Mata starting together for the first time. But United's luck was not in, and first-half injuries to Phil Jones and Jonny Evans forced Michael Carrick to fill in at centre-back with

Rooney moving back into midfield, scuppering all tactical plans made for a blustery Britannia Stadium.

The Potters duly moved ahead via a large slice of fortune as Charlie Adam's wayward free-kick was heavily deflected past a stranded David De Gea. Van Persie – released by Mata – managed to restore parity after the break with a confident finish past Asmir Begovic, though the Reds were level for only five minutes before former Blackpool midfielder Adam doubled his tally with a wind-driven effort that flew straight into the top corner from range. 'It was a difficult day, the conditions were tough,' explained a frustrated David Moyes after the final whistle. 'We had opportunities to get at least a draw and they scored a world-class second goal which was hard to defend against.'

Rene Meulensteen's bottom-of-the-table Fulham were up next at Old Trafford, where United fell behind to Steve Sidwell's 19th-minute strike in front of a shell-shocked Stretford End. Despite controlling 75 per cent of the possession in a match that was one-sided from start to finish, the Reds failed to make a breakthrough until the 80th minute when two goals in as many minutes from van Persie and Carrick appeared to secure a morale-boosting victory. But deep into added time, substitute Darren Bent headed a dramatic equaliser that stunned Old Trafford and its re-trialled Singing Section into silence, capping another highly frustrating outing for fans on the terraces. As the *Telegraph*'s Henry Winter wrote, the Reds' approach was just a little too orthodox. 'United have a great history of wing play but they overindulged here, putting in 81 crosses, the most by a team in the Premier League since 2006, but only 18 of which went to team-mates. Such tactics played into the hands of Maarten Stekelenburg and his defenders, who dealt comfortably with the hosts' bombardment.'

After two disappointing results, a trip to Arsenal wasn't exactly the ideal fixture – even if the Gunners had just received a 5-1 drubbing at Liverpool. Nevertheless, Moyes instructed his players to 'harness the hurt' and Carrick was determined to set matters straight at the Emirates Stadium. 'Of course we care about results,' said the midfielder. 'No one wants to go through a spell when people are questioning you and things are going wrong, but we have had enough success over the years that we retain a belief in ourselves, even when things are not going so well.'

Such faith led to a much-improved performance in North London that yielded an encouraging if uneventful goalless draw, which would have been so much more had van Persie's late header not been palmed onto the crossbar by Wojciech Szczesny. After the final whistle, the typically mild-mannered Carrick spoke out again, this time defending his midfield colleagues after a solid display. 'We get stick all the time anyway, but we're used to it. I thought we did a good job – not just us in midfield but as a unit, really. We hoped for a little bit better, we'd hoped for a win. But it shows we're not such a bad team – we just need to get back to playing like that and get the wins.'

Moyes and his squad flew to much warmer climes and a week-long training camp in Dubai; a shrewd move ahead of a daunting trip to relegation-threatened Crystal Palace, who were flourishing under the tutelage of new manager Tony Pulis. Having landed back home with just under 24 hours until kick-off at Selhurst Park, a further boost was provided by the announcement that Rooney had signed a new four-year contract that would also make him a club ambassador upon his retirement. The long-serving striker was determined to push on and bring the good times back to United, saying: 'This is a new era for the club. We have some great players and despite our recent form everyone has stuck together and the team spirit is good. We will continue to work hard and get Manchester United to the top where it belongs.'

In the end, United made relatively light work of Palace and

secured a comfortable 2-0 win thanks to van Persie's second-half penalty and Rooney's sumptuous half-volley that left fans and pundits purring. While it wasn't a spectacular display, this was definitely a step in the right direction. Without ever suggesting that talk of a decline was premature, United moved up to sixth with a first victory in three matches and the win was given added gloss by a spectacular clincher that underlined Rooney's continued importance at Old Trafford.

In keeping with the season's one step forward and two back approach, more pain was just days away – and it would hurt much more than before. Away to Olympiacos for a Champions League tie that looked entirely manageable on paper, United were completely overwhelmed by the Greeks and succumbed to a lacklustre 2-0 defeat via goals from Alejandro Dominguez and Arsenal loanee Joel Campbell. The result sent ripples around Europe and, afterwards, Moyes acknowledged his side deserved to lose in Piraeus but refused to blame just his players. 'There's undoubtedly talent at Manchester United but tonight we didn't show it,' he told reporters. 'Me and the team, we didn't show it together. I take responsibility. It's my team and I'll always front up. The players are hurting as well. They know how they performed. We're a team and we stick together.'

Player of the Month – Juan Mata

While it was by no means a stellar month in terms of results, club-record signing Mata managed to impress during his four outings to win February's player of the month award, suggesting United were right to break the bank for his services. With three assists to his name, the Spaniard was understandably pleased by his hugely promising start to life at Old Trafford: 'It's amazing for me to be awarded with this prize after my first month. I have played just a few games and I am really grateful the fans have voted for me,' he explained. 'I feel really happy. Life in Manchester is good, I have already found a house, I have a new home and I am trying to know different places around the city. It is a really nice city to live in. It is quiet, relaxing and you can be focused on what is important – playing football.'

Game of the Month – Crystal Palace 0 United 2, Premier League

In context, United's trip to Crystal Palace was an unquestionable highlight that provided cause for optimism. The game had been preceded by the announcement of Rooney's new four-year contract, which brought a definitive end to lingering rumours of a potential move to Chelsea. A three-match winless streak in the league was also brought to end via an impressively comfortable 2-0 win, set up by van Persie's penalty and Rooney's exquisite second-half volley. Fit-again midfielder Marouane Fellaini also made a positive impact on his first start since early December. After the match, Moyes was full of praise for his No.10. 'I said to everyone from day one that Wayne came in and has trained well,' said the Scot. 'He's never been a problem and credit should go to the owners and the board for making a stand to keep the best players. We're building a new team, we're keeping the good players and we'll be adding to it.'

Goal of the Month – Wayne Rooney vs Crystal Palace

With the news agenda being dominated by the announcement of Rooney's new contract, it felt inevitable that United's No.10 would provide some justification at Selhurst Park. When it came, it was well worth waiting for. Patrice Evra's cross pinged across the edge of the area with pace, though Rooney had no intention of controlling it. Instead, with relish in his eyes and his head over the ball, he swung a clean right boot through the ball to beat Julian Speroni with an exquisite strike. Understandably, the scorer was delighted by his finish. 'I just tried to do well for the team and to help us win,' he said. 'Whether I've signed a new deal or not, I always try and give one hundred and ten per cent on the pitch and that's what I did. For my goal, the ball was set up nicely. I knew that if I got decent contact on it, I had a chance.'

March

A nightmarish opening to 2014 had bottomed out during the chastening defeat to Olympiacos, and there was only one way for the Reds' campaign to go. The first springboard back to acceptable standards was provided by West Bromwich Albion at The Hawthorns, where a dominant display gave David Moyes's men three much-needed points. Phil Jones's bullet header opened the scoring, but it was a pair of sublime goals from Wayne Rooney and Danny Welbeck, both of which followed extensive passing moves, which provided the greatest cause for optimism.

'It is a confidence-booster,' admitted Rooney. 'We were hurt after the Olympiacos game, and we needed to go out and show everyone that we are a good team. We'll fight for the shirt, and we'll fight for a place in the team, and I think that showed today. We played with a great energy, we were exciting and we always looked a threat, so I think we deserved the three-goal win. And it could have been more.'

With Premier League games against title-chasers Liverpool and Manchester City straddling the Champions League decider against Greece's finest, the stakes could hardly have been higher. 'It's a big month ahead, we're well aware of that,' conceded Michael Carrick. 'It's Liverpool next and that's a big one. I don't think league places affect the game. We'd say it if we're top of the table that form goes out of the window against Liverpool, it counts for very little, and that's the case now.'

Unfortunately, Brendan Rodgers' on-song Merseysiders were too strong and strolled to a 3-0 win at Old Trafford in a remarkable game in which Steven Gerrard netted two penalties and missed another, before Luis Suarez capped a miserable afternoon for the ten-man Reds, who lost skipper Nemanja Vidic to a red card in the second half. 'It's one of the worst days I've ever had in football,' said a shell-shocked Rooney.

The need to bounce back emphatically was clearly evident ahead of Olympiacos's visit to Old Trafford. 'The players are capable of turning it around,' insisted Moyes, of his side's two-goal deficit. 'We're all desperate to put things right and make sure we play better to give the supporters here something to shout about. We have to go for the throat to get the win.'

'Like the manager says, it's really important we score early on Wednesday,' echoed Patrice Evra. 'When you come to Old Trafford and concede an early goal, it's difficult. I'm confident. I'm not selling a dream and saying we will definitely qualify. There are too many words right now. We just have to show on the pitch. That is most important.'

Sure enough, United required just 45 minutes to level the tie on aggregate through a Robin van Persie brace, and the Dutchman curled home a free-kick to complete his hat-trick after the restart, taking the Reds into the quarter-finals on one of the outstanding nights of a difficult campaign.

'This football club is capable of it,' smiled Moyes. 'If we play to our capabilities, which we've not shown that often this season, I think we can be a match for any team. I don't want to say this is the moment, but in the same breath I really hope it is. It was a really good result in Europe as we came from two-nil behind. We hadn't played well in the first game but we put it right. The result means we've got ourselves another two games in the Champions League. That's something we'll really look forward to.'

The mood was tempered slightly by the news that hat-trick hero van Persie had sustained a knee injury which would rule him out for much of the rest of the season, while the daunting spectre of reigning European champions Bayern Munich loomed large in the quarter-finals.

Van Persie's absence was not immediately costly, however, as Rooney strode to the fore with a memorable brace to secure victory at West Ham. His first goal was a headline-maker, a thumping lob from near the halfway line which quickly evoked comparisons with David Beckham's famous 1996 effort against Wimbledon. 'It was just instinct,' said the striker. 'I've turned and I've had a quick look and seen the goalkeeper off his line. It's one of those that I've tried many times and I was delighted with that.'

Much like Rooney's lob, United's fortunes had crested and, after successive wins, were soon on the downturn. Manchester City's visit to Old Trafford began in nightmarish fashion, with Edin Dzeko scoring inside a minute, and the Bosnian's second-half header and a late Yaya Toure goal wrapped up a comfortable win for the visitors.

'City started very fast, we lost a goal after forty or so seconds and because of that we were on the back foot right away,' admitted Moyes. 'The players know exactly what it is to play for Manchester United – they know the standards they have to set. But they're hurting as well as me and are desperate to put it right. And hopefully when we get to the game against Aston Villa, they can show that.'

Despite the concession of an early Ashley Westwood free-kick, a pair from Rooney, Juan Mata's first goal for the club and a late Chicharito tap-in secured a convincing victory for the hosts – providing a welcome boost ahead of April's Champions League summit with Bayern Munich.

Player of the Month – David De Gea

Speaking at the start of March, United's Spanish No.1 said: 'I've been happy with my form and I've felt very confident. I've played a lot of games, learned a lot and gained consistency and stability. I'm pleased with how things are going.' Fortunately for the Reds, he didn't just talk a good game. In a month of mixed collective fortunes, the 23-year-old was a model of consistency, posting clean sheets against West Brom, West Ham and Olympiacos. His most telling contribution was a stunning double save which allowed the Reds to overturn a two-goal deficit against the Greek champions, after which the *Daily Telegraph*'s Jim White wrote: 'The Spaniard was magnificent, probably more influential in the final result than any other player on the pitch.' Further to his Champions League heroics, De Gea also manfully kept a lid on the scorelines in the one-sided home defeats to Liverpool and Manchester City.

Game of the Month – United 3 Olympiacos 0, Champions League

With a clear mission set out before the game, the Reds knew that something special would be required to overturn a two-goal deficit to extend their involvement in the Champions League. Sure enough, one of the season's best displays was served up. Van Persie took the plaudits and the match ball for his decisive hat-trick, but it was the efforts of the ageless Ryan Giggs which led to the Reds' first two goals and set the scene for a memorable comeback. 'He defies his age,' said the Welshman's manager. 'He was fantastic, the passes he made, his general football, and his fitness. Normally you think with a player like that you need to bring them off at sixty minutes, but not him. He's a freak.'

Goal of the Month – Wayne Rooney (1st) vs West Ham United

While there was an aesthetic excellence to the team goals scored by Rooney and Danny Welbeck at West Brom, there was simply no topping the former's stunning individual effort at Upton Park later in the month. Latching onto Ashley Young's hooked pass, the striker levered Hammers midfielder Mark Noble out of the way before, fully 50 yards from goal, opting to smash a lofty lob at the hosts' goal. As goalkeeper Adrian back-pedalled and tangled himself into a heap on the ground, the ball arced towards the target. 'I did worry that it might bounce over the goalkeeper at first, but you just have to hope for the best,' admitted the striker, who then grinned: 'Thankfully it came off.' And with that – and with two months of the campaign remaining – the book was shut on United's Goal of the Season award.

April

Having suffered two morale-sapping home defeats to Liverpool and Manchester City in late March, United were clear underdogs when European champions Bayern Munich arrived at Old Trafford. Even club Ambassador Gary Neville, who was part of the 1999 Treble-winning team that knew no fear, was understandably cautious before kick-off, admitting: 'I'd say, going into this game, we're hopeful rather than confident. That's just being realistic – Bayern are at the absolute top of their game. You're talking about a team at the absolute peak of its powers, while Manchester United is in transition.'

In the end, against the grain of expectations, United produced a dogged performance to hold the Germans to a gutsy 1-1 draw following Nemanja Vidic's second-half header and a clipped finish from Bastian Schweinsteiger, who was later sent off for a second bookable offence that ruled him out of the second leg in Munich. Despite controlling just 30 per cent of the possession, David Moyes's men were much improved and could have secured a shock win, had Danny Welbeck's early goal not been harshly disallowed for a high foot before the Longsight lad wasted a glorious opportunity by chipping straight at Manuel Neuer when clean through. 'It was not the massacre of Old Trafford that the club might have feared,' wrote the *Independent*'s Sam Wallace. 'Catastrophe was averted, Dignity remains intact. United are still very much alive for the return leg at the Allianz Arena which, in the new era of lowered expectations, is as much as they might have hoped for.'

With confidence restored, United travelled to Newcastle for an apparently taxing fixture in the North-East but, with a much-changed team, the Reds punished Alan Pardew's men to clinch an emphatic 4-0 win. Juan Mata, ineligible to play in Europe, was the star and made the most of his opportunity by scoring a brace of goals (including a delicious free-kick to open the scoring) before strikes from Javier Hernandez and Adnan Januzaj wrapped up a resoundingly positive afternoon at St James' Park.

The only sour note was a first-half injury to Ashley Young, who was immediately sent to hospital for scans on a dislocated thumb, but that would not dampen the manager's spirits. 'I'm thrilled by our away performances,' Moyes explained, when asked about United's top form on the road. 'We just need to try to show that more at Old Trafford. The hardest thing in football is probably winning away from home. Expectations at Old Trafford are really high but some of the football we played today was fabulous.'

A flight to Bavaria followed as United landed in Munich for the second leg with Bayern, who were missing Schweinsteiger and fellow midfielder Javi Martinez through suspension. Wayne Rooney was also an injury doubt, having missed the trip to Tyneside with a bruised toe, though Pep Guardiola was willing to bet reporters 'a large glass of beer' on the talisman's inclusion. The Spaniard was later proved right as Moyes revealed his cards at a pre-match press conference. 'We've taken advice from the doctors and the people who advise us,' he explained. 'Everybody knows the type of character Wayne is and he is determined to play. If he is determined we would be mad not to give him that opportunity.'

Poignantly, on the eve of the tie, Moyes led an emotional visit to the Munich Air Disaster memorial site, which is now named 'Manchesterplatz' in honour of the passengers who tragically died on the runway in 1958. Surrounded by his players, the boss laid a wreath at the granite stone that featured 58 red roses and one white rose for each of the 23 victims. Michael Carrick later described the visit as a 'moving experience', which also provided a timely reminder of what Manchester United stands for – strength, courage and overcoming adversity.

All of those attributes were required at the Allianz Arena and, perhaps inspired by history, United produced a gallant performance. For the matter of seconds which followed Patrice Evra's stunning second-half strike, the Reds even dared to dream the impossible dream. But in the euphoria of scoring, concentration lapsed and Mario Mandzukic darted into the area to instantly restore parity from Franck Ribery's cross. The Germans then moved up a gear, going ahead in the 68th minute through Thomas Muller before Arjen Robben's deflected shot inflicted a frustrating 4-2 aggregate defeat. After the match, a weary Moyes was determined to lead his team back in the competition, even if that wouldn't be until the 2015-16 season. 'There's no shame going out to Bayern Munich – they are a good side,' he told reporters. 'The players have played really well. We'll show the quality we've got, re-group and start building towards being back in the competition.'

However, the time that Moyes craved was running out and his next match, a brutal trip to former club Everton, would prove to be his last as United manager. Goals from Leighton Baines and Kevin Mirallas did the damage at Goodison Park as the Reds succumbed to a lacklustre 2-0 defeat that made it mathematically impossible to finish in the top four. Although Moyes spoke candidly about improvements and transfer plans after the final whistle, he was relieved of his duties just two days later as the club released this short statement: 'Manchester United has announced that David Moyes has left the Club. The Club would like to place on record its thanks for the hard work, honesty and integrity he brought to the role.'

Ryan Giggs was duly named interim manager for the four remaining games of the season, with fellow Class of '92 graduates Paul Scholes, Nicky Butt and Phil Neville joining him as coaches. After a 'whirlwind week', the Welshman held his first press conference as boss at the Aon Training Complex and explained just what the job meant to him. 'I've got to say it's the proudest moment of my life,' he told the media. 'I've supported Manchester United all my life and it's been the biggest part of my life since I was fourteen when I signed schoolboy forms. I'm proud, happy, a little bit nervous but just like I am as a player I can't wait for the game on Saturday.'

The spectacle certainly lived up the occasion. Norwich City were the opposition and neutrals were right to feel sorry for the Canaries, who couldn't have faced United at a worse time. Old Trafford was bouncing, buoyed by the sight of a suited and booted Giggs, appealing every decision and kicking every ball from the manager's technical area. In the end, despite a sluggish start, the Reds were rampant and secured a galvanising 4-0 win thanks to braces from Rooney and second-half substitute Mata, whose exclusion from the starting XI was just one of the reasons why Giggs endured a sleepless night prior to kick-off.

While this victory was of little importance to the season, with nothing to play for except pride, it was at least restorative. It was a throwback and, above all else, a release. Having entered and departed to a hero's ovation, Giggs discussed his newly inherited team with great honesty and ambition. 'They're all good players and all of us have let ourselves down this year,' he said. 'We haven't played to the level that we're capable of this season, but we did that today. I said yesterday that it can't just be for one game, it has to be for longer than that. Every time you play for Manchester United you have to stay at that level, and they have to keep to these standards.'

Player of the Month – Juan Mata

United's record signing was cup-tied for the Champions League glamour ties with Bayern Munich and subsequently made just three domestic appearances in April, though the diminutive Spaniard made the most of his limited game time and enhanced his reputation by scoring a couple of superb braces against Newcastle and then Norwich. The second was particularly impressive as it was wrapped up in just 30 second-half minutes, after he came off the bench to give Giggs plenty to think about during his first match as interim manager. For United's big-money signing, the 2014-15 season could not come soon enough. 'I think we are all looking forward to next season,' he admitted. 'Obviously we want to win the last games but we are looking forward to improving and a better season than this one. I want to bring success back to these supporters, because I think it is what they deserve.'

Game of the Month – United 4 Norwich City 0, Premier League

In a tumultuous month of enormous upheaval, the outstanding afternoon was steeped in familiarity. In terms of sheer romance and history, the sight of club legend Giggs walking out at Old Trafford as Manchester United manager takes some beating. For those lucky enough to attend, this was an 'I was there' moment that was

24 seasons in the making. The stadium was engulfed by a feel-good factor and after a rousing reception that made Giggs feel 'ten feet tall', United got to work. Following a timid start that was perhaps the result of an emotional week, the Reds produced an incisive attacking display that yielded an encouraging 4-0 win thanks to doubles from Rooney and Mata. As for Giggs, he was determined to finish a chastening season on a high. 'They've just told me that I've got this job for four games,' Ryan explained. 'I'll do the job to the best of my ability and then afterwards we will have to see what happens.'

Goal of the Month – Patrice Evra vs Bayern Munich

But for Wayne Rooney's March wonder-goal at West Ham, Patrice Evra's awe-inspiring thunderbolt in the Allianz Arena would have walked to the Reds' Goal of the Season award. Over to Pat: 'It was an emotional day, the day before the game. Everyone had been to the Munich memorial, where the plane had crashed with the Busby Babes. It was amazing. I was talking with a young player like Adnan Januzaj and telling him that these people were like us, they were on a plane going to play a football game. And at the end they never saw their families again. I always pray before games, but I asked, "Can I give something for the Busby Babes?" I didn't say a goal but just to make sure we played for them in that game. That's why when I scored that goal, you can see I was really emotional, I was angry. I couldn't believe it. That was my little secret – and now everyone knows that secret.'

May

As the final month of the 2013-14 campaign began, all talk was of Ryan Giggs. After inspiring a rousing return to form against

Norwich, the Reds' interim manager was looking ahead to the visit of relegation-battling Sunderland while also fielding questions about his own future as a player.

'Nothing has changed – it's until the end of the season and we'll chat when that's over,' he flat-batted the queries. 'My main concentration is on Sunderland and the remaining two games [against Hull City and Southampton]. I'm still training and doing bits and pieces so I'm still in the frame on maybe playing in the remaining games. I'm just trying to keep myself fit and trying to win every game. I might not get back into the team!'

That possibility was duly dashed, however, when Gus Poyet's resurgent team left Old Trafford as worthy winners, courtesy of Sebastian Larsson's first-half strike. For Patrice Evra, a limp display from the hosts summed up a frustrating season. 'This year has been a season to forget really quickly,' he conceded. 'It's been so painful – it's not just about this game. Sunderland were fighting for their lives and deserved to win. It's about lots of games.

'We have been really poor and deserved all the criticism because we didn't play well enough and lost some stupid games. That is why we are in this position. Everyone failed and that is the point. My mentality, you know, is never to give up but it's been really bad and we have to take responsibility – each player. The senior players and the younger players. That is it.'

With one more home game to consider, the Reds' temporary manager opted to shake up his approach and named a squad which blended youth and experience. The oldest player (Giggs himself) was older than his two debutants (James Wilson and Tom Lawrence) put together, and all three played a part on an emotional evening at Old Trafford.

Wilson converted a pair of close-range finishes to become only the 13th player ever to score more than once on his United bow, and later admitted: 'It was a great feeling, you can't compare it to anything else.' Giggs, meanwhile, emerged from the bench to assist Robin van Persie's late clincher in a 3-1 victory. Afterwards, both the interim manager and departing skipper Nemanja Vidic addressed the crowd to recognise their sustained support, and the Serbian's impending transfer to Inter Milan prompted plaudits from within the Old Trafford dressing room.

'You want to win the game but, at the same time, you've got to celebrate Vida,' said Michael Carrick. 'We have to celebrate the service he's given the club for so long, having achieved so much. He's a leader and one of the best defenders the club has had. It's sad that he's leaving because he'll be missed as he's a top player and an important part of the squad. Sometimes you've got to move on and we respect that.

'I'm sure he must have been touched by the reception he got from the crowd. He's a man of few words so I was a bit surprised to see him get on the microphone at the end. You could see he was touched and there was definitely some emotion there. He's got one game left, but that was his last one at this special place. He'll be missed.'

There remained the small matter of one final outing for Vidic, Carrick and company: the season finale at Southampton. The Serbian ended the afternoon in customarily combative fashion, shedding blood after a clash with Rickie Lambert but soldiering on as Juan Mata's sublime free-kick earned the Reds a 1-1 draw in a hard-fought game.

The final whistle marked the end of Giggs's interim tenure, and he would soon also confirm the end of an epic playing career, but his involvement with his boyhood club was sustained by his installation as assistant to Louis van Gaal, who was announced as the Reds' new manager on a three-year contract shortly after the end of the season.

'We have secured the services of one of the outstanding managers in the game today,' said executive vice-chairman Ed Woodward. 'Everyone is very excited about this new phase in the club's history.

His track record of success in winning leagues and cups across Europe throughout his career makes him the perfect choice for us.'

'It was always a wish for me to work in the Premier League,' added van Gaal, who would commence his new role after completing his World Cup commitments with the Dutch national team. 'To work as a manager for Manchester United, the biggest club in the world, makes me very proud. I have managed in games at Old Trafford before and know what an incredible arena Old Trafford is and how passionate and knowledgeable the fans are. This club has big ambitions; I too have big ambitions. Together I'm sure we will make history.'

Player of the Month – Adnan Januzaj

As one of the undoubted bright spots of United's season, the Belgian youngster capped a superb debut campaign with strong outings in each of May's games. Adnan was one of few players to threaten Sunderland during a second-half cameo, before he shone with adventurous 90-minute displays against both Hull and Southampton, with the latter providing an engaging tussle with future Reds team-mate Luke Shaw. 'Adnan is a great lad,' said interim manager Giggs. 'He wants to learn. He wants to get better. He wants to improve. That is great to see. He is a talent.'

Game of the Month – United 3 Hull City 1, Premier League

In a month of few contenders, the emotional victory over Hull City provided the unquestioned highlight of the season's tail-end. While a glimpse at the club's future provided promise, the game will take its place in history as the 963rd and final game of Giggs's career – even if the man himself felt different. 'Obviously I managed to get on the pitch, but I think the main memory will be the youngsters coming on and doing so well,' he insisted. 'Manchester United always give young players a chance and it's up to them to take it. They certainly did that.'

Goal of the Month – Juan Mata vs Southampton

A spirited second-half fightback at St Mary's should have yielded victory for the Reds, but ultimately the only route past Saints goalkeeper Artur Boruc was a sublime free-kick from the club's record signing. Akin to his similarly brilliant effort at Newcastle in April, the Spaniard took aim from the right-hand side of the area, trotted casually up to the ball and, with minimal back-lift, clipped an unstoppable effort into the corner of the goal. 'It was an important goal but not enough to win which is what I wanted,' lamented the 26-year-old.

Meet the Manager: Louis van Gaal

It takes a special kind of manager to cope with the sporting behemoth of Manchester United, especially in the modern age. The need to win, and win with style – while factoring in sky-high expectations, commercial demands and an ever-present spotlight – heaps incredible pressure on the incumbent. Louis van Gaal possesses the character and skill to handle all those demands.

In appointing the Dutchman as manager, United selected a candidate with an outstanding record of success amassed with some of world football's grandest institutions: Ajax, Barcelona and Bayern Munich as well as the Netherlands national team. A UEFA Champions League and UEFA Cup winner, plus a league champion in three different countries, the then-62-year-old arrived at Old Trafford on the back of leading his country to an unexpected third-place finish at the 2014 World Cup in Brazil.

Long renowned as a larger-than-life character, van Gaal is a teacher, a philosopher and, inevitably, a complex personality who has taken on the biggest job in English football with relish and gusto. One of nine siblings, he grew up in the Watergraafsmeer neighbourhood of Galilei Park, Amsterdam and enjoyed a fruitful amateur career as an attacker with local side RKSV De Meer. He came to the attentions of Ajax, his boyhood team, and joined them at the age of 18.

A huge stroke of misfortune placed Louis in direct competition with future Netherlands great Johan Cruyff for a starting berth, and he found his route to the first team blocked before moving to Belgium to join Royal Antwerp in 1973. Even at a young age, van Gaal had also studied to become a gym teacher, and he continued to juggle his education with his on-field commitments after a move back to Holland with Sparta Rotterdam. Having returned home, he began to broaden his horizons with a part-time teaching role in an Amsterdam high school.

Education provided an enormous part of his younger life. As a teenager, Louis had watched legendary Dutch coach Rinus Michels mould Ajax's exceptional youngsters on the training field and, having subsequently been on the club's books during their three successive European Cup triumphs, he had absorbed a wealth of knowledge. He was fluent in winning, and it was time to translate it to others. By the time his career came to an end at AZ Alkmaar, he briefly took on a youth coaching role with the club, before becoming the manager of Ajax's famed academy.

Back at his boyhood club, Louis soon began to climb the career ladder and, having assisted coach Leo Beenhakker, became first-team manager after his forebear's departure to take the Real Madrid helm in 1991. He required time to succeed, but made the most of his intimate knowledge of the club's fruitful youth system to promote from within, with staggering effects. His third season yielded the first of three successive Dutch league titles, while Ajax also bagged the UEFA Cup and UEFA Champions League in successive seasons, before becoming world champions in 1995.

Ronald De Boer, one of those hand-reared starlets, reserves only praise for his former manager: 'For me, he was an amazing coach. If you look back through the names in that team – Van der Sar, my brother [Frank], Overmars, Kluivert, Davids, Seedorf – you think: "All those players are stars." But at that time we weren't stars, we were just up-and-coming stars. Van Gaal worked well with younger players and he was telling us which direction we should go. He did it with so much passion and belief so we followed him. And he was always right.'

Not for the last time, van Gaal's success in Holland would pave the way to a huge move abroad, as Barcelona came calling, intent on ending a run of three years without a La Liga title. The Catalans immediately won back-to-back championships, yet a second-place finish in his third term prompted his departure to manage the Dutch national team, where an unexpectedly unsuccessful stint prompted a brief return to Camp Nou. There was also a return to Ajax as technical director after his swift second departure from Catalonia, but it was van Gaal's 2005 move to AZ Alkmaar that prompted one of his greatest achievements in management. Louis led the club to second and third in successive seasons, but planned to resign after finishing 11th in his third term, until his players demanded that he reverse his decision and remain in charge for the 2008-09 campaign. The result was AZ's second-ever league title, secured by an 11-point margin from Steve McClaren's FC Twente.

Once again, success in the Eredivisie led van Gaal to a European goliath; this time Bayern Munich. Having blooded Xavi, Carles Puyol, Victor Valdes, Andres Iniesta and Thiago Motta during his two stints at Camp Nou, van Gaal continued to provide a launchpad for future stars by handing debuts to unknown teenagers Thomas Muller, Holger Badstuber and David Alaba. Despite such a radical overhaul of an established side, Bayern overcame a slow start to surge to an unforgettable Double triumph – with van Gaal becoming the first Dutch manager to win the Bundesliga title. But for defeat in the Champions League final by Jose Mourinho's Internazionale, Louis would have taken Bayern to their first Treble in his maiden season.

Less than a year later, however, the Dutchman had left the Allianz Arena amid a disagreement with club president Uli Hoeness. For the third time, he returned to a former employer, this time relishing a second tilt at international management. The ghosts of his first term were exorcised with emphatic qualification for the 2014 World Cup, where van Gaal's Netherlands later made a mockery of low expectations by obliterating reigning world champions Spain en route to an impressive third-place finish in Brazil.

By that time, his appointment as United's incoming manager had been confirmed, with Ryan Giggs installed as his assistant within a backroom set-up which included several new Dutch arrivals. Having spent almost his entire playing career working under Sir Alex Ferguson, Giggs conceded that there are parallels between van Gaal and British football's greatest manager.

'I do see similarities,' said the Welshman. 'They have an aura about them. That comes from the success they have had. They demand the players respond and they demand respect. In the short space of time I have worked with him, you can see why he has been a success. He is infectious. Everything he does is clear and everyone gets it straight away. He has got a unique way of putting it over, but it's brilliant to see. It's quite simple, but if you make a mistake he will tell you and if you do something good he will tell you. This is a philosophy the manager believes in and that he has had a lot of success with – his CV speaks for itself. He has managed at big clubs and he is coming into the job off a successful World Cup, so already he has shown what he can do and I think the players have responded to that.'

Another member of the new-look coaching staff, opposition scout Marcel Bout, has been working with van Gaal since his first stint at Ajax, and sees the manager's philosophy as the realisation of a football ideal. 'I think his way of working is the most difficult way of working you can imagine,' said Bout, 'because he likes to play football – nice football – and win prizes. When you compare that philosophy with other coaches, and I've seen a lot, they are playing in a way which does not take too much risk but trying to get the highest result. Louis wants to take risks and in the way he has done that he has won a lot of cups – you can see that from his statistics. I think the way he wants to play is difficult and beautiful as well. Nowadays a lot of coaches are reacting, but Louis wants to create. That's the big difference.'

Wherever he has been, van Gaal's impact has lasted beyond his presence. His fingerprints indelibly adorn the coaching careers of modern greats Jose Mourinho and Pep Guardiola, who both worked with him during his time at Barcelona. His penchant for fielding youth-team graduates has yielded fruit long after his departure, and he remains dedicated to giving young talent its chance at Old Trafford.

'Every youth player who is coming up is a guardian of the culture of the club,' he said. 'He learns the culture from the age of a child. The Class of Ninety-two were guardians of the culture of the club. So it's very important a club such as Manchester United has guardians and therefore you need very good youth education so you have always more players who can be used as a guardian in this club. I have done that with Barcelona and Munich. I want to do that also here, but the youth player has to take their chance when they receive it.'

Therein lies the key to van Gaal's appointment at Old Trafford: the recognition of existing traditions but the absolute devotion to maintaining standards appropriate of such an institution. With a relentless, proven winner at the helm, United can realistically harbour hopes of short-term success and long-term stability.

Meet the Coaching Staff

The appointment of Louis van Gaal also prompted a reshuffle of the Reds' backroom staff, with a wealth of established expertise making its way to the Aon Training Complex to aid the new manager in his quest for success.

Ryan Giggs, assistant manager

For United's all-time leading appearance maker, 2014 was an eventful year. Having stepped up to replace David Moyes as the Reds' interim manager, he brought down the curtain on football's most successful playing career and was immediately installed as Louis van Gaal's assistant manager.

Speaking in the early weeks of his role, the Welshman admitted: 'It was a great opportunity for me and I am loving it. Obviously a coach's work is done before training, after training and during training as well, so it is different from being a player when you are just focused on training. I have been analysing games, presenting to the players and it has been a good learning experience. A lot of the coaching courses teach you to take yourself out of your comfort zone because that will improve you. Some of the things I have been doing have been out of my comfort zone but I have really enjoyed it.'

Having only taken on his first player-coach role under Moyes in the 2013-14 season, Giggs's experience on the 'other' side of the touchline is varied, but limited. His fellow coaches, however, were quickly impressed by his aptitude behind the scenes. Van Gaal swiftly declared: 'I'm very pleased with Ryan. My first impression of him was already good, and it keeps improving. You have to work very hard when you're my assistant – it's not always a pleasant job! But he's doing well, very well and I'm very happy he's on my staff.'

A substantial portion of Ryan's role is to deliver scouting reports to his former team-mates, piecing together research provided by analysts Marcel Bout and Max Reckers, and the latter underlined how impressed he had been by the Welshman's ability to embrace change. 'He's unbelievable,' said Max. 'There is so much new technology coming at him, but he managed everything straight away. We have been amazed, he is doing fantastically well.'

In his time working under van Gaal at Barcelona, Jose Mourinho was handed similar duties to Giggs, and the Welshman has made no secret of his desire to make a future career in management. According to his fellow coaches, the potential is very much there.

'According to Louis's philosophy, it's normal that there is a legend in his staff at United and Ryan maybe wants to become a future Manchester United manager, so it's a good thing for him and for United that he's in our staff,' said Bout. 'He played nearly a thousand games for Manchester United so we are not just talking about a former player, he is a legend. He is learning to become a manager and from what I've seen over the last few months Ryan can be a very good one in the future.'

Albert Stuivenberg, assistant coach

Feyenoord's Academy, which provided several members of the Netherlands squad that excelled at the 2014 World Cup, is renowned as one of world football's finest breeding grounds of young talent. In Albert Stuivenberg, United appointed a man who worked within that remarkable education system for 22 years as a coach. Having previously had a promising career with Feyenoord cut short by injury at the age of 18, Albert studied for the next three years before returning to the club in a coaching capacity, in which he remained until the summer of 2014. It was his moonlighting with the Netherlands youth teams, however, which first prompted him to cross paths with Louis van Gaal. 'I was coach of the Holland Under-17s and was quite successful there, winning the European Championships twice, and last season I was the Under-21 coach,' said Stuivenberg.

'We worked together very closely. I had a lot of young players who were candidates for the Dutch national team, so we discussed these things a lot and got to know each other quite well. We found that our views on football were very similar. He got an idea of who I was, and decided I was the right man for the job – I was honoured, but also very happy with the challenge we now face.

'I'm very honoured to be here and to be a part of this fantastic club, and I've also got the chance to work with one of the best coaches in the world. Looking at his experience and the things he has won, you can only learn, so I'm very happy with the situation.'

The respect is clearly mutual, with van Gaal remarking: 'He has so much talent, this boy. I picked him up in the Dutch federation, he did a remarkable job and that's why I want to reward him to be my assistant here as a coach.'

Stuivenberg's work in Manchester will involve working closely with Ryan Giggs and Marcel Bout on the preparation of training sessions, and meetings between the coaching and playing staff. Feedback for players is also a key part of his role, with squad members briefed and debriefed either side of every game.

'We think it's very important that the players know what we expect of them,' said Albert. 'We give them a lot of information and feedback, both positive and negative. We work from a structure that we absolutely believe in and that has been successful in the past, and the players have responded very positively. We get feedback from them, and we have been happy with that, and hopefully this will be the first step in becoming a winning team again.'

Frans Hoek, goalkeeper coach

One of the most established, respected goalkeeper coaches in the game, Frans Hoek has worked with Louis van Gaal since 1989, when the latter arrived at Ajax.

Hoek, who was already tutoring the club's goalkeepers across all age bands, worked with van Gaal every day during the latter's subsequent reign as boss before joining him in his move to Barcelona. Frans remained at Camp Nou after the manager's resignation three seasons later, and was around for van Gaal's second stint at Barca before departing to work with the Polish national team.

The pair reprised their relationship at Bayern Munich in 2009 and continued it with the Netherlands national team before moving to Manchester in tandem. Inevitably, they have long since been singing from the same hymn sheet.

'I think we are both searching for perfection,' said Hoek. 'I think that's more common in goalkeeping coaches than regular coaches because of the effect a mistake can have as a goalkeeper. We look forward to the science of teaching and developing players, we complement each other in the things we do, and working with Louis means working at the highest level. It's always going for the biggest

Man of the Match David De Gea saves a penalty from Leighton Baines in United's thrilling 2-1 victory over Everton in October.

Rafael hurdles the challenge of Morgan Amalfitano during the Reds' win over West Ham United on 27 September.

Luke Shaw is congratulated by manager Louis van Gaal after United had beaten Liverpool in Miami to win the International Champions Cup.

Phil Jones showed his ability and adaptability in United's crucial 1-0 victory over Arsenal in November 2013.

Marcos Rojo gets some advice from skipper Wayne Rooney during a training session at the Aon Complex on the day after his signing had been announced.

Jonny Evans showed some of his best form as United went in pursuit of their 20th league title in 2012-13. Chelsea's Demba Ba has no answer to the Reds defender's power and commitment.

Angel Di Maria celebrates scoring *Match of the Day*'s September Goal of the Month, a stunning chip against Leicester City.

Juan Mata scores one of two sublime goals against Newcastle United in April 2014, but his efforts couldn't prevent the Reds from falling short in the race for a Champions League place.

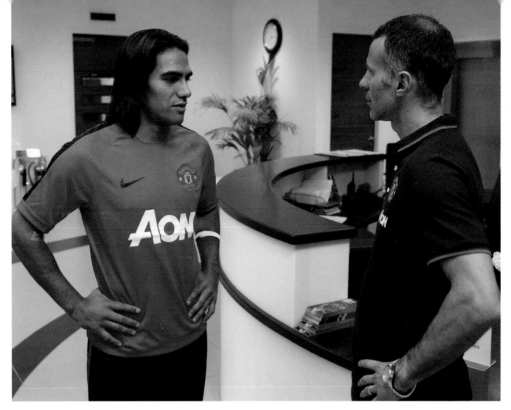

Who better to show Radamel Falcao what United is all about than Ryan Giggs? The Colombian striker had the perfect guide on his first day at the club.

Wayne Rooney, the latest proud wearer of the captain's armband for United, urges on his team.

Adnan Januzaj scored twice against Sunderland in October 2013 on his starting debut for the Reds – two efforts that made everyone take note of the 18-year-old.

Under the watchful eye of Louis van Gaal, Chris Smalling goes through his training routines during United's 2014 summer tour of the United States.

Anders Lindegaard warms up ahead of United's Capital One Cup semi-final decider against Sunderland in January 2014.

Michael Carrick moves the ball on, despite pressure from Arsenal's Mesut Ozil. Gunners boss Arsene Wenger is one of many admirers of United's quietly effective midfielder.

Daley Blind put in a superb performance against Queens Park Rangers in September to show United fans that the late transfer-window signing was a top-quality acquisition.

The arrival of Louis van Gaal at United gave Ashley Young a new role during the summer tour, which he clearly relished, turning in a Man-of-the-Match performance against Real Madrid in Ann Arbor.

prizes at the biggest clubs, so it feels good together. Whenever he asks me to work with him, I always say yes, so I think we have a good understanding.'

Frans's role is specifically to work with the club's stable of goalkeepers. Having been credited with playing a major role in the early development of modern greats Edwin van der Sar and Victor Valdes, the Dutchman is to adopt a broader view than purely focusing on senior stoppers David De Gea and Anders Lindegaard. 'They all have a role,' he stressed.

The coach's protégé, van der Sar, demonstrated a masterclass in the art of goalkeeping during his time at Old Trafford, ensuring that the vast majority of opposition attacks were snuffed out before true danger could rear its head. Prevention over cure was the Dutchman's mantra, and Hoek stresses that the subtleties of goalkeeping come into play at United, where the No.1's contribution extends far beyond repelling countless shots.

'We know that at a club like United, where usually you are stronger than your opponent, the goalkeeper will work a lot less in general,' said the coach. 'They have to act less, but the quality of the actions they do has to be better. The key to goalkeeping is concentrating from the first second until the last, and even then I believe you are focused until you get back to the dressing room after the final whistle.'

With one of the game's most esteemed coaches now overseeing their work, United's clutch of stoppers are primed for a fascinating chapter in their education.

Marcel Bout, opposition scout

A specialist in developing young talent and scouting opponents, Marcel Bout is another hugely experienced addition to the United backroom staff. He sporadically crossed paths with Louis van Gaal during the manager's spells with Ajax and Barcelona, but it wasn't until 2006 that the pair first worked together on a full-time basis at AZ Alkmaar.

Marcel's role in AZ's success prompted van Gaal to insist that he reprise their relationship at Bayern Munich, and once again silverware followed. So highly rated was Bout at Bayern that he was retained on the coaching staff after van Gaal's departure. The pair were soon reunited, though, working closely again in the Dutch national set-up, with Bout a key member of the country's Under-21 backroom team and the senior side's 2014 World Cup campaign.

Having worked so regularly with van Gaal, Bout has been struck by the manager's open-mindedness while remaining true to his long-standing philosophy of football. 'He is a coach who makes it clear what he wants,' said Marcel. 'He has been explaining a lot to the players, as he wants to get his philosophy across and that takes time. There are a lot of coaches who work in a certain way and try to keep that going in the same way, but every day Louis wants to know everything about new things. He tries to implement that into his philosophy, he is always looking at trying to use any new things.'

In the perpetual quest for any advancements or information which can make a fraction of a percent's difference in United's favour, a sizeable part of Bout's role is to provide van Gaal with detailed breakdowns of opponents. 'Fifty or sixty percent of my role is going "on tour" to compile match reports on our next opponents,' he said. 'At the end of the game I write a report, but during the game I am already thinking what we possibly can do to beat the opponents.'

Despite his vast experience, including his stint at German superpower Bayern, Marcel conceded that he was stunned by the size of United upon his arrival at the club. 'I spoke to Ed Woodward and he asked me what Dutch people thought of Manchester United,' he recalled. 'I told him that in Holland we thought United is a rather big club, and he told me: "Wait until you see it and wait until you feel it." I can say now it's not a big club, it's a huge club!'

Max Reckers, statistical analyst

United's already impressive sports science department, which is responsible for the statistical analysis of the club's players, was embellished by the addition of Max Reckers on the insistence of Louis van Gaal. 'He's not only my computer guru,' laughed the boss, 'he's also nearly my son! Max collects all the data that we need, and we have a lot of data because in Manchester United, already there was a philosophy that you have to measure everything.'

Reckers first came into contact with van Gaal when he joined AZ Alkmaar as a video operator. 'I convinced Louis that we could take another step,' Max recalled. 'We immediately found that there was so much more than just video; tracking systems came in and training started to get more emphasis. We became champions in our second year there and Louis went to Bayern and wanted to continue the process, so we did. We had two very successful years there before Louis joined the national team which obviously ended at the World Cup with a successful third-place finish.

'The manager is a very innovative person. He wants to know how these things work, so he's really involved and we spend a lot of time together. It developed at Bayern Munich and his wife has been my second mother, just as Louis has been a second father to me.'

Reckers' research is a cornerstone of the Reds' meticulous planning. He is primarily responsible for the feedback which each player and the team as a collective receives. He spends matches watching play and requesting clips from video operators, and is able to immediately access the footage to provide instant feedback wherever required. The information he compiles also forms the spine of the post-match debrief for individuals and the group. The wealth of data accumulated could be seen as daunting, but Max thrives on the challenge.

'All the information comes to me and I make sure everyone gets the data they need,' he said. 'We need a lot of equipment. During the match we use a lot of video cameras, as well as tracking systems which follow the movements of the players and the ball. Those give you a new level of data which we then process and use to give feedback.

'We keep innovating, meaning that we demand that the players improve themselves every day and the same goes for the staff. Every day we are looking for new technologies and new ways to improve player performance. For us, it's not doing science or having the technology, it's just wanting to improve as a group.'

Pre-season Tour 2014: United States

Sat before the world's media during his first press conference as Manchester United manager, Louis van Gaal took a question from the floor about his decision to take only two days' rest following the World Cup in Brazil. 'This is a big challenge, a big ambition for me,' the Dutchman explained, with typical consideration and intensity. 'When there is a challenge like this, I never let it go. This is a holiday for me!'

Just 24 hours later, having taken a tour of Old Trafford with Sir Bobby Charlton, an experience he described as a 'great honour', van Gaal was aboard another long-haul flight to take charge of the Reds' extensive pre-season tour of America. While a three-week trip around the States may sound appealing, van Gaal meant business and quickly got to work with United.

Double training sessions were ordered and, aided by assistant manager Ryan Giggs and a backroom team comprising several newly recruited Dutch coaches, the boss set about moulding the club in his own image. Having cast a learned eye over the 23-man travelling squad, focusing on the attributes of each player, a decision was made that United would line up in a 3-5-2 formation. While the system was completely new to everyone, particularly the defence, it would produce an emphatic result from its inaugural outing.

Under the glow of the California sunset, United romped to a 7-0 victory over LA Galaxy thanks to goals from Danny Welbeck, Wayne Rooney (2), Reece James (2) and Ashley Young (2). The match in Pasadena was particularly impressive for the fact the hosts were halfway through the MLS season, rendering this much more than a pre-season tune-up against an unfit opponent. The Americans were sharp and ready to go. As such, the Reds drew much confidence from the run-out and van Gaal was pleased by the way his team adapted to a new formation after just two 11 vs 11 training matches. 'It's fantastic how they have performed,' smiled the Dutchman. 'When you see us train, you can expect something but not a seven-nil win. It was a surprise, but they were all beautiful goals and beautiful attacks.'

Ander Herrera also made his unofficial debut that night and shone as part of a midfield triumvirate that included Darren Fletcher and Spanish compatriot Juan Mata. With 90 minutes under his belt, not to mention the approval of Reds supporters around the world, the former Athletic Club star was understandably enthused by his first outing. 'It was a dream for me to play in the red shirt – I will keep this shirt with me always. I hope this is the start of a lot of games for United,' he said. 'It wasn't only me in this game, though, I think the whole team enjoyed the game and did well. It's the first match and we have done good things. It's a good step and we're very happy.'

A trip to Denver followed, for the start of the International Champions Cup, a tournament in which eight of Europe's top teams split into two groups with a place in the Miami final up for grabs. United's first match was against Italian giants AS Roma at the Sports Authority Field, home to the Denver Broncos, where high altitude levels (5,280 feet above sea level) made life difficult for the players. Thankfully, a breathless start helped the Reds build an emphatic 3-0 lead via goals from Juan Mata and a brace from Wayne Rooney

– whose opener was a genuinely world-class strike from around 30 yards. Miralem Pjanic then pulled one back after the break with another spectacular strike from well inside his own half, before Francesco Totti added a late penalty to seal an entertaining 3-2 win for United. The only sour note was the 11th-hour decision to send Rafael home for treatment on a groin injury.

Nemanja Vidic's Inter Milan were up next and the Reds' former captain, who left the club at the end of the 2013-14 season, admitted beforehand that it would be surreal to face United following nine glorious seasons at the Theatre of Dreams. 'It's good that it's a friendly match,' he said. 'I wouldn't love to play against United in a competitive game. It will be strange playing against players I trained with and against a club I was part of for so many years. But in another way, I will be glad to see friends.' In the end, Vida's defensive strength proved difficult to overcome and a frustrating goalless draw led to United sealing a 5-3 penalty shootout victory at the FedEx Field in Washington DC.

The Inter game was also notable for Luke Shaw's second-half introduction for the injured Reece James, given that the summer signing had been told to improve his fitness by van Gaal. The England international was relaxed and quick to explain the situation. 'I totally agree with the manager,' the 19-year-old admitted. 'To play in this formation, as a wing-back, you have to be really fit. I am fit but I am not at the high level the manager demands. I have got to get fitter to get up and down, and it's something I have got to work on.'

With one foot in the final, United travelled to Michigan for a meeting with European champions Real Madrid and a fixture that never fails to capture the world's attention. Indeed, the match was broadcast to over 40 nations and played before 109,318 fans at the appropriately nicknamed Big House stadium. The attendance was a record for a 'soccer' game in the US, beating the 101,799 who saw the 1984 Olympic gold medal decider at Pasadena's Rose Bowl. The most important statistic is always the scoreline, though, and a 3-1 victory over Carlo Ancelotti's men left Reds supporters purring. Ashley Young maintained his excellence pre-season form with another brace of goals, which sandwiched Gareth Bale's first-half penalty. Javier Hernandez stepped off the bench to score a decisive goal that teed up a mouth-watering final with Liverpool in Miami.

Despite both managers insisting this was a game that carried little significance as a pre-season friendly, van Gaal and Anfield boss Brendan Rodgers still selected their strongest available team for the first meeting of England's most successful clubs on foreign soil. Wearing the captain's armband for the night, Wayne Rooney did his hopes of securing the role on a permanent basis no harm by inspiring a dramatic fightback after his neat volley early in the second half cancelled out Steven Gerrard's first-half penalty opener. Juan Mata then gave United the lead before substitute Jesse Lingard's 88th-minute strike secured a 3-1 win and a first trophy of the new era.

Having overseen five successive victories while on tour, van Gaal was understandably optimistic about the new season and what his team might achieve. While also pleased to be lifting silverware at the first opportunity, the Dutchman maintained focus on more pressing matters at hand. 'It's nice for the fans in the USA and also at home that we beat Liverpool. I think we gave a lot of pleasure to the fans and that's very important.'

Player of the Tour – Wayne Rooney

'He's always a winner,' van Gaal stated, when quizzed on Wayne Rooney being named Player of the Tournament following the International Champions Cup final in Miami. 'I think he deserved to win the award, because he made a lot of assists and scored five goals. But we also defended well – there are a lot of defenders who could also have been the most valuable player of this tournament.' As the boss explained, United's success in America was down to a strong team ethic and willingness to learn. Tyler Blackett earned praise at the back, Darren Fletcher and Ashley Young were much-improved in midfield, while Juan Mata was exemplary behind the striker.

Game of the Tour – United 3 Real Madrid 1

Scoring seven goals against any opponent is special, as is beating bitter rivals Liverpool when trophies are up for grabs, but United's impressively comfortable win over Real Madrid cannot be overlooked when it comes to tour memories. Although Carlo Ancelotti had chosen to play safe by not starting Cristiano Ronaldo, with recent £63 million signing James Rodriguez and French forward Karim Benzema missing from the tour altogether, victory over the Champions League winners was still an impressive scalp for the Reds. This was also a box-office occasion for the Michigan college town of Ann Arbor and its enormous stadium, where tickets for the fixture sold out within a day of going on sale. The crowd was the biggest that United had played in front of since the 1957 European Cup semi-final against Real at the Estadio Santiago Bernabeu, when 120,000 turned out to see the home side defeat the great Busby Babes.

Goal of the Tour – Ashley Young (1st) vs Real Madrid

From a purist's point of view, Ashley Young's opener during the 3-1 win over Real was a goal of rare beauty. Following a cagey opening to the game, the United winger finished off a stunning move of 20 passes in which Darren Fletcher played a key role. Having received the ball from Antonio Valencia, the Scotland midfielder broke forward before passing to Wayne Rooney on the edge of the penalty area. Rooney's back-heel to Danny Welbeck saw the ball moved on to Young and the England winger beat Iker Casillas from 12 yards to prompt a roar of delight inside the Big House. 'Broadcasters all over the world should show the first goal by Young – it was a fantastic goal,' van Gaal enthused afterwards. 'I think all the team touched the ball in the build-up. People could have come to the stadium just for that goal, I think.'

2014 – A Summer of Change

By the end of the 2013-14 season, which yielded United's worst league finish since 1990, there was little doubt that wholesale changes would sweep through Old Trafford – though few could have foreseen the scale of the transfer business which made the Reds the summer transfer window's highest rollers.

It all began in May with the initial appointment of Louis van Gaal, whose first engagement as boss was a meeting in an Amsterdam hotel with new assistant manager Ryan Giggs. 'When we met at the end of last season, we went through the players who are here and some of the players he liked that will maybe come in. Two have already come in,' the Welshman later revealed, referring to Ander Herrera and Luke Shaw, the former Athletic Club and Southampton stars who signed within 48 hours of each other in late June. 'He knew a lot, as you might expect,' Giggs continued. 'But any little thing I could help him about, I tried to. We didn't dwell on what happened last season.'

Despite the squad requiring extensive surgery following the departures of Rio Ferdinand, Nemanja Vidic and Patrice Evra, not to mention Giggs himself, van Gaal was initially reluctant to enter the market and offered his existing squad a chance to shine during the pre-season tour of America. 'My method is always the same. I want to look at the players now, who are here at present,' he said. 'Of course I know how the players play, but I don't know how the players play once I have trained and coached them. The first three or four weeks, I want to see what they can do. Then, maybe I will buy more players.'

In the end, the manager afforded his squad more time to catch the eye and did not sanction any business until late August, barring the mid-tour capture of 17-year-old goalkeeper Vanja Milinkovic. The real action began 11 days before the end of the transfer window, with the purchase of Sporting Lisbon's Marcos Rojo, whose arrival saw Nani go the other way on a season-long loan. Real Madrid superstar Angel Di Maria signed on the dotted line for a club and British record fee of £59.7 million just six days later, before Ajax midfielder Daley Blind was reunited with his former Netherlands manager on deadline day.

Just as fans were sitting back to reflect on a very active window, the club confirmed the 11th-hour arrival of Radamel Falcao on a long-term loan from Monaco. There was also time for 16-year-old Dutchman Timothy Fosu-Mensah to sign from Ajax, completing a transfer window that stunned the football world and set tongues wagging in the Reds community. Before long, the tabloids heralded an age of the 'Gaalacticos'.

Of course, room needed to be made to accommodate the newcomers, and supporters bade farewell to several familiar faces over the summer. Bebe and Alexander Büttner were first to leave, for Benfica and Spartak Moscow respectively, before Shinji Kagawa was sold back to former club Borussia Dortmund.

That deal was soon followed by the high-profile departure of local lad Danny Welbeck, who joined Arsenal just hours after fellow Academy graduate Tom Lawrence moved to Leicester City. Nick Powell also joined the Foxes as one of many loan deals that also saw Javier Hernandez (Real Madrid), Tom Cleverley (Aston Villa), Wilfried Zaha (Crystal Palace), Mike Keane (Burnley) and Angelo

Henriquez (Dinamo Zagreb) all leave the club on a temporary basis.

With his squad suitably trimmed and styled more to his taste, van Gaal set about turning his new collection of players into a team and, brilliantly, earned instant post-window results with the 4-0 annihilation of Queens Park Rangers. The performance was slick, imaginative and powerful; attributes that excited both the manager and the fans alike.

A brighter future, it seemed, would follow the summer of change at Old Trafford. 'I said before the game: "Let us make a new start,"' the boss revealed after beating QPR. 'That's very important for us because, after the transfer period, we can now work on a team-building process and make ourselves better every week.'

Leases of Life

Several members of United's first team squad will spend all or a portion of the 2014-15 season out on loan at other clubs. Whether they are youngsters honing their craft or established professionals in need of regular action, here are the Reds who have gone out on loan this term . . .

Tom Cleverley

Aston Villa, Premier League, England

Having risen through the United ranks to become a regular for both club and country, Tom Cleverley realised a lifelong dream by becoming a Premier League champion with his boyhood club in 2012-13. Thereafter, however, his Reds career waned as he came in for disproportionate criticism for the team's collective shortcomings in 2013-14, and a raft of new arrivals under Louis van Gaal presented the opportunity for the England international to move to fellow top-flight side Aston Villa.

The Villans had stiff competition from Everton for Cleverley's temporary signature, and the midfielder concedes that, with his

United contract due to lapse at the end of 2014-15, there is no guarantee of what the future holds. His focus must remain short term, however, as he bids to rediscover his top form by playing regularly. Doing so would provide Paul Lambert's team with an invaluable addition; after all, Cleverley was labelled 'potentially the best midfield player in Britain' by Sir Alex Ferguson in 2012.

'Football is a game of opinions and you can't please everyone,' said Tom. 'Louis van Gaal was always straight with me. I had a fairly good pre-season where we won every game, but he has his own players. The manager made it fairly clear it wasn't going to happen for me [at United]. It is something I had prepared myself for. In modern football it is rare that one player, like Giggsy or Scholesy, plays for one club for their whole career.'

Angelo Henriquez

Dinamo Zagreb, Prva Liga, Croatia

Now aged 20, two years after joining United from Universidad de Chile, Angelo Henriquez has been on the Reds' radar since he was 14 years old. A lethal goal-getter for the youth ranks of his club and country, the Chilean sharpshooter united the Reds' army of scouts who watched him.

'Everyone said: "You need to bring him in,"' revealed Sir Alex Ferguson, who signed Henriquez in 2012. 'He's very quick and a good finisher. He's strong, with great shoulders on him for a boy. So hopefully he'll do fine.'

The 2014-15 term will be spent in Croatia at Dinamo Zagreb, with Angelo embarking on his third loan spell in as many seasons since moving to Manchester. A half-season stint with Wigan Athletic in 2012-13 preceded a successful season-long spell with Real Zaragoza in 2013-14, in which he scored six times in 20 starts. With his route to the United first team blocked by Wayne Rooney and Robin van Persie, plus new signing Radamel Falcao and the up-and-coming James Wilson, the decision was taken to send the Chilean to Zagreb.

His assimilation to life in Croatia's top flight could hardly have gone better, as he bagged a 94th-minute debut winner against Dinamo's fierce rivals, Hadjuk Split, to become an instant fans' favourite with his temporary employers. Sustained first-team football will provide Henriquez with the platform to showcase the unerring finishing which first brought him to United's attention as a teenager.

Javier Hernandez
Real Madrid, La Liga, Spain

'It is a dream come true,' said Javier 'Chicharito' Hernandez after moving to the reigning European champions on a season-long loan. 'There is no player in the world who would say no to Real Madrid if they came in for them. Obviously, I have always been a fan of this club.'

Few would begrudge Hernandez the chance to resurrect his career on such a grand stage. One of the most popular figures around the club on account of his sparkling personality, Chicharito enjoyed four rollercoaster seasons at Old Trafford after arriving as a virtual unknown in the summer of 2010.

He soon altered that with a stunning debut campaign in which he played a major role in the Reds' 19th league title triumph and earned the Sir Matt Busby Player of the Year award. A deadly finisher but also a consummate professional, Hernandez soon found himself being utilised as an impact substitute, and his ability to play the role to perfection – scoring 17 goals from 69 introductions from the bench – ultimately counted against his case for regular starts.

Another invaluable scoring contribution in 2012-13 brought a second title in three seasons for the fleet-footed Mexican, but he found opportunities hard to come by under the management of David Moyes and, when Louis van Gaal arrived in Manchester and assessed his striking department, the decision was taken to make Chicharito available on loan.

His dream move to the Estadio Santiago Bernabeu materialised in the form of a one-year loan deal, but Los Blancos have the option to make the deal permanent in the summer of 2015 if they wish.

Mike Keane

Burnley, Premier League, England

Spend time with Mike Keane and one thing that becomes abundantly clear about the polite, intelligent youngster is his straightforward single-mindedness. There is no arrogance, no edge and certainly nothing flash. This is a player who is interested in just one thing: making it at Manchester United.

Along with twin brother Will, the 21-year-old Stockport lad has been immaculately raised by a family whose support has proved crucial during his rise through the Academy. But as he so eagerly points out, he's far from finished. 'They have obviously seen the hard work that has gone into it; it has not all been smooth and we have had patches when things weren't going so well. They have helped me get to where I am today, but we have to recognise there is a lot more work to do to kick on again.'

To help this process, Mike has agreed to join Premier League new boys Burnley until at least January 2015 in a bid to absorb knowledge of English football's top division. However, moving away is nothing new for him. The 2011 FA Youth Cup winner is something of a rolling stone following previous temporary spells at Derby County, Blackburn Rovers and Leicester City – where his inspired form even earned him one of three places on the Foxes' shortlist for their Player of the Season Award.

The ultimate aim is, naturally, to cement a place in Louis van Gaal's starting XI. 'This is arguably the perfect time to be a young player at Manchester United,' Mike insists. 'The manager doesn't have any problems throwing young players into big games. It's good to be around.' In the short term, Keane will ply his trade in Lancashire, with a view to impacting upon his return to the Reds.

Nani
Sporting Lisbon, Primeira Liga, Portugal

At the outset of his eighth season at Manchester United, Nani found himself on the periphery of Louis van Gaal's plans and was soon aboard a flight back to former club Sporting Lisbon as part of the deal that brought summer signing Marcos Rojo to Old Trafford. Going back isn't necessarily going backwards for the Portuguese, who dazzled for the Primeira Liga side until United snapped him up in 2007; it actually provides an opportunity to regroup and rebuild following a two-season spell that was plagued by injury and inconsistency.

Nani is capable of the truly magnificent and can mesmerise the world's top defenders on his day. This was most unquestionably evident during the title-winning 2010-11 season, when his outstanding form (10 goals and 18 assists in 49 appearances) led to his colleagues voting him their Players' Player of the Year at the club's end-of-season awards night.

Fitness and form issues clouded his subsequent campaign, and 2012-13 is best remembered for a controversial dismissal during United's Champions League last-16 second-leg defeat to Real Madrid at Old Trafford. The following term was similarly frustrating for the wing wizard, with chances at a premium under David Moyes, who often put his faith in young Adnan Januzaj when selecting wingers.

Now back in his home town, the city of his creation, Nani hopes to reclaim the form that made him one of the world's top forwards. 'I am back to revive my career,' he said upon arrival. 'Returning home I can say that I'm happy to be back. I'll be close to my family and friends. I can say I feel good.'

Nick Powell

Leicester City, Premier League, England

Just moments after Nick Powell's first-team debut, in which the talented youngster scored the final goal in an emphatic 4-0 win over Wigan Athletic in September 2012, Sir Alex Ferguson revealed just one of the reasons why he personally scouted the young Englishman before sanctioning his transfer from League Two outfit Crewe Alexandra.

'Powell is going to be a really good player who, we hope, will fill Paul Scholes's boots,' said the Reds' former manager. 'He's got terrific vision, good temperament, two great feet, is quick and is a great striker of the ball.' While this was an apparently bold statement, given the magnitude of Scholes's legacy in M16, Ferguson's belief in this rough diamond was resounding.

After a maiden season that produced six senior appearances, including two in the Champions League, Powell spent the following term on loan at Wigan and scored 12 goals in 42 appearances for Uwe Rosler's side – who just missed out on promotion from the Championship. His form at the DW Stadium inspired another ringing endorsement – this time from his temporary boss.

'What excites me about Nick is he can play everywhere,' explained Rosler. 'He can come on as a midfielder, then I put him up front and, in many games, I play him in a wide position coming inside and I can play him as a number nine because he has a tremendous physique.'

Powell has since continued his ascension by joining Premier League side Leicester City on a season-long loan, enhancing his education at the highest level. 'I could have gone to the Championship and played week in, week out – but the Premier League is the next step I need to take,' said the England youth international, whose unquestioned talent now has to show itself on the highest domestic stage.

Wilfried Zaha

Crystal Palace, Premier League, England

Although Wilfried Zaha's first-team opportunities have been few and far between at United, the England international remains an exciting prospect for the future and hopes to make a lasting impact at Old Trafford following his season-long loan at former club Crystal Palace.

The London-raised winger, who was born in Ivory Coast, left the Eagles for United in January 2013 but was immediately sent back to Selhurst Park to finish an already promising campaign. The decision, made by Sir Alex Ferguson, proved to be a masterstroke after Ian Holloway's side secured promotion to the Premier League, with Zaha later claiming the Championship Player of the Year award.

He then returned to United, though playing time under Ferguson's successor, David Moyes, was unfortunately limited and so a short-term switch to Ole Gunnar Solskjaer's Cardiff City was sanctioned in the second half of 2013-14. While Zaha was unable to fly the Bluebirds clear of relegation, the experience of fighting the drop proved vital for this precocious talent. 'I've realised there are things about my game I need to work on and concentrate on,' he said. 'I know this [United] is the best place to be if I want to improve. I really want to make myself a better player.'

Despite such a positive attitude, new manager Louis van Gaal struggled to accommodate the youngster in his 3-4-1-2 formation – mainly because the system operates with wing-backs instead of traditional wingers – and Wilf was loaned back to Palace once again to continue his development.

'United is a great club, but since I've gone up there it hasn't gone my way, really,' he explained. 'I haven't really had the chance to showcase my talent or play much – that's why I thought it would be best for me to get a loan, gain some experience and maybe go back a better player.'

The 2014-15 Squad Profiles

1. DAVID DE GEA

Position: Goalkeeper
Born: 7 November 1990; Madrid, Spain
Previous club: Atlético Madrid
Joined United: 1 July 2011
Debut: 7 August 2011 vs Manchester City (N), Community Shield
Honours: Premier League (2012-13), Community Shield
(2011, 2013)

With slender shoulders and a gangly frame, David De Gea was a soft target for criticism when he arrived at United in June 2011, tasked with the unenviable job of replacing the great Edwin van der Sar. Now, having weathered the storm that clouded his first season in England, in which a host of experts openly questioned his acquisition, the Reds' undisputed No.1 is on the brink of greatness after making history at the end of the 2013-14 campaign.

Having kept 19 clean sheets behind an unsettled defence, and amid the vast upheaval of coaching staff, the 23-year-old became the first-ever goalkeeper to win the prestigious Sir Matt Busby Player of the Year award, beating off competition from Wayne Rooney and Adnan Januzaj as fans recognised his impressively consistent form between the sticks. His team-mates also followed suit, crowning him their Players' Player of the Year to complete a remarkable double for the Spaniard.

Such has been the rise in De Gea's stock, he then capped a season of personal success by replacing the injured Victor Valdes in Spain's 2014 World Cup squad. Though a leg injury ruled him out of a disastrous campaign for La Roja, who were surprisingly knocked out of Group B after just two matches, the young glovesman has nevertheless come a long way in a short space of time and seemingly has the world in his safe hands.

From an early age, quiet confidence has been De Gea's trump card. Prior to his unexpected debut for Atlético Madrid – as an 18-year-old deputy for injured second-choice keeper Roberto – David had already won over manager Abel Resino. 'I spoke to him about it. He said to me: "I'm better than all the other goalkeepers here. I'll get in the first team here." There was something I liked about him. There was assuredness, security. It wasn't arrogance, it was conviction.'

That self-belief convinced Atlético to pull the plug on a deal to send De Gea on loan to Wigan Athletic. In fact, those at the Estadio Vicente Calderon soon realised they had a unique prospect on their books, according to renowned Spanish journalist Guillem Balague. 'People were talking about Joel Robles as the prominent goalkeeper coming through their ranks. Atlético Madrid went along with that to protect De Gea because they knew that he was something special. As soon as he came into prominence, everyone saw his potential and there was no doubt that he was going to go far.'

Products from Atlético's own cantera are always popular on the terraces and, after a series of mediocre performances by first-choice goalkeeper Sergio Asenjo, fans were calling for De Gea by the end of 2009. His chance duly arrived and he took it emphatically. A star in high-profile games against Barcelona and Real Madrid, in addition to Atlético's successful Europa League run of 2009-10, David's twinkling talent quickly caught the eye of United. So, in the summer of 2011, he was enlisted to replace the retiring van der Sar at Old Trafford. The Dutchman's legacy could hardly have been more intimidating, but Sir Alex Ferguson, scarred by the lengthy and painful process of replacing Peter Schmeichel, was certain he had the right man (or boy) for the job. Having passed up chances to sign Petr Cech and Joe Hart in previous years, citing their tender age as his reason, he would not make the same mistake again.

In spite of De Gea's obvious potential, the British press sensed blood and quickly set about questioning his claim to Edwin's throne. He was too young, too small and unable to handle the physical demands of the Premier League according to many. Admittedly, a poor start didn't help his case. Beaten by Edin Dzeko's speculative effort in the Community Shield and Shane Long's altogether tamer shot in United's Premier League opener at The Hawthorns, the Spaniard was pounced upon by trigger-happy critics. 'The goalkeeper is like a jelly,' said one experienced scribe. 'I can't see what he's got. How on earth Ferguson and all his millions of coaches could have watched this boy week in, week out and then signed him I just don't know.'

The Spaniard initially shared goalkeeping duties with Anders Lindegaard, until an ankle injury forced the Dane onto the sidelines in late January 2012. Less than a week later, De Gea enjoyed a watershed moment in his Reds career. Having reeled in Chelsea from a three-goal deficit to level at Stamford Bridge, parity was preserved by a staggeringly athletic fingertip save to flick away Juan Mata's injury-time set-piece. 'From a personal perspective that was important,' David later admitted. 'When you look back over a season, there are lots of defining moments and key goals. Particularly from a personal point of view, the fact the save was right in the last minute was decisive. Possibly it gave me a huge confidence boost as well.'

Though his debut campaign ended on a collective low, with United losing the title to Manchester City on goal difference in the final seconds of the season, De Gea had gained invaluable experience. He was virtually ever-present throughout 2012-13, keeping 12 clean sheets in 41 appearances as United claimed a 20th English league title in Sir Alex's final season as manager. The highlights were numerous, but few match up to his mesmerising display of agility in February's Champions League draw at Real Madrid, when a single swipe of his right foot denied a Fabio Coentrao shot to keep United in the tie. Alas, despite its brilliance, his unorthodox style was still questioned on English soil – but not in Spain.

'Like always when someone tries something new, people say: "You're wrong. For a hundred years we did it this other way,"' says Balague. 'David uses his feet for saves, sometimes with his feet elevated to the same height as his hands, which has created a bit of controversy in England, but I think he may be onto something here. There's a lot of intuition and preparation in it. He told me that if he sees that a save with the hands is not going to have enough power, the foot will always take the ball away from the danger area. David does it systematically as part of his weaponry.'

As you might expect by now, De Gea was suitably unruffled by both his performance and the praise it attracted around the world, maintaining supreme calm and composure throughout the repercussions. At this point in his career, according to former goalkeeping coach Eric Steele, he was able to take the rough with the smooth. 'Any criticism goes off that quiff,' Steele explained at the Bernabeu. 'That is the great thing about David. He's able to say: "Right, fine." He might have dark moments but he keeps them away from the training ground. If he is ever hurt, he doesn't show it. If you think about what David has been through, he has to have inner strength. He has dealt with it. He hasn't come in swearing and squeaking. He's just got on with his job. He's very mature for his age. He's had to be because you're not just replacing a goalkeeper in Edwin, you're replacing a legend.'

Sir Alex walked away from management in May 2013 and David Moyes was immediately hired as his successor, prompting a significant reshuffle of United's backroom staff in which Steele lost his job. A new era was at hand. But before any of that, De Gea was aboard a flight to Israel for the UEFA Under-21 Championship, where his flourishing Spanish team-mates would retain their title won in Denmark two years earlier with a stylish 4-2 victory over Italy in the Jerusalem final. The United stopper also made history by receiving his 27th cap with the age group, equalling the all-time appearance record originally set by assistant manager Santi Denia.

Upon his return to United, De Gea began working under Chris Woods, his new goalkeeping coach. The former England No.1 soon realised that he was working with a player far removed from the one who had arrived in M16 two years earlier. Substantially buffeted and buffed, he was not only a champion but the realisation of potential. 'Previously I was watching him from the outside the club, so then going from that to working with him have been two totally different scenarios,' explained Woods. 'The first things that struck me were his calmness and his all-round natural ability. Beyond that, he doesn't get flustered – although I have seen him throw his gloves over the fence once – and calmness is good because if you look uneasy or like you're rushing things, it doesn't breed confidence.'

As the Reds floundered on the pitch, with results continuing to go sour under the new manager, it became increasingly apparent that De Gea would be one of the few figures who would end a chastening campaign with an enhanced reputation. Having banished the mistakes that undermined his early career, the 23-year-old was demonstrating his established reflexes, agility and speed of thought with unquestionable authority and consistency.

Stunning saves were made at vital times, most notably to deny Sunderland's Emanuele Giaccherini at the Stadium of Light before a game-changing double stop inspired United's escape act against Olympiacos.

Encouragingly, for United fans at least, the Spaniard's thirst for improvement remains unquenched. 'He's still so young,' said Woods. 'They say goalkeepers improve with age and maturity, and I don't think you ever stop learning. He listens and takes things on board. He wants to keep learning every day. That's so important because the time that you think you know everything is the time that you stand still.'

De Gea's aforementioned awards double was recognition of his new standing at Old Trafford, where his long-term future looks a few shades brighter than sunny. With 132 appearances registered at the start of the 2014-15 term, the fans' favourite can realistically break records with the club. 'I must say, David has gone up another notch,' said 1968 European Cup winner Alex Stepney, whose 539 outings remains the zenith for goalkeepers at United. 'He has taken his game to another level and it's been great to watch him develop here at Manchester United. I pay close attention to him during matches, and he is communicating a lot with his back four – that means a lot to the defence.

'He's commanding his area too, and that shows you the development he has made. His handling of the ball is excellent and he commands that six-yard box brilliantly, and that's the great thing he has brought into his game. It's interesting as well when you think how well he has done this season that the back four in front of him has rarely been the same back four. He's done very well to organise the four in front of him and still keep so many clean sheets.'

Although often uninterested by praise and attention, favouring the quiet life instead, De Gea has intriguingly discussed the notion of overtaking Stepney's longstanding milestone. 'The record is a lot of games,' he recently admitted. 'You never know, though. At the moment, that figure seems very high but I'll take it one game at a time. I hope to play as many games as I can for Manchester United and, who knows, maybe one day I will reach that number and go even higher.'

Given what David De Gea has already achieved in his short career, few would bet against him.

2. RAFAEL

Position: Defender
Born: 9 July 1990; Petropolis, Rio de Janeiro, Brazil
Previous club: Fluminense
Joined United: 1 July 2008
Debut: 17 August 2008 vs Newcastle United (H), Premier League
Honours: Premier League (2008-09, 2010-11, 2012-13), FIFA Club World Cup (2008), League Cup (2009-10), Community Shield (2008, 2011, 2013)

From the foothills of Petropolis to the peak of the Premier League, Rafael da Silva has undergone a lengthy journey in his football career.

Having signed for United in 2008 along with his twin brother, Fabio, the tenacious, energetic full-back has grown from a boy into a man during his time at Old Trafford. Now a husband, father and veteran of over 150 first-team outings, the 24-year-old has come far. Born and raised in Petropolis, a scenic, undulating city in the state of Rio de Janeiro, Rafael and Fabio's upbringing centred around two pillars: family and football. To this day, nothing has changed.

'Nothing else matters,' said Rafael, with a customary glimmer of mischief in his eye. 'Growing up in our village, we just enjoyed life. It was so good. They were moments when you just didn't care for anything. There was so much to do, just playing with other kids. They are great memories. It's funny – we played football but lived in the hills, so we put flip-flops down as goals on both sides, and one played up the hill and the other played down the hill. It wasn't easy ... Much better to be playing down the hill!'

Football was in the da Silva blood, after their father Jose had enjoyed a successful amateur career and their elder brother Ricky had made it to the brink of the professional game with Brescia in Italy. It was the twins who made the leap, however, starting in the youth ranks of Brazilian top-flight side Fluminense, even though it meant moving away from home at the age of just 11.

'I couldn't even look them in the eye,' admitted their father. 'They went up the hill [to Fluminense's training facility] and they were waving. Even today it still gets me. They were only small, walking up that hill to the academy. When I left I was so sad. My heart was aching. I said to them: "Look, we may be suffering, but tomorrow it will be worth it."'

Those words ultimately proved prophetic when the pair were scouted by United four years later, but the twins' subsequent trials in Manchester and agreement to join Sir Alex Ferguson's side in the future irked Fluminense, who barred them from training for a year before their departure to England.

'It's a long story ... a bad story,' sighed Rafael. 'They stopped us from playing because we had agreed to come to United. In the end, before we came to England, we weren't training or doing anything at Fluminense. We were invited over to United to train, but Fluminense told us not to do that, that instead we should stay and spend six months or one year in their first team. United accepted everything, then Fluminense changed their minds and we ended up not playing at all.'

The situation did, inevitably, impact on the boys' progress – visibly so in their early days in Manchester. 'It was so bad,' laughed Rafa. 'I don't know what United thought they had signed! After the first few sessions you could tell people were thinking: "These aren't the guys we had here before." After a while, though, we got back to normal.'

Having officially arrived and joined up with Ferguson's first-team squad ahead of the 2008-09 season, the twins were given their first public outing in a pre-season friendly at Peterborough, with Rafael starting and Fabio joining the fray as a substitute. 'To be honest, as soon as I arrived here and signed my contract, I said: "I am here and now I am going to play for Manchester United. I have to play here,"' recalled Rafael. 'I always said this to my brother: "I have to play for Manchester United." I remember that game at Peterborough because it was so important. We both played and it was a good game. I think that was the game where United started to think: "Ah, OK, they can be Manchester United footballers." I always feel happy when I remember that game, because it was the start.'

Perhaps that was true for Rafael, who turned in a sensational, all-action performance which left onlookers enraptured. Fabio's more understated outing left him trailing his sibling in the race for first-team action, and Rafa quickly became a regular squad member for the reigning European champions. He impressed Ferguson, most of all after putting in a magnificent substitute's display in a defeat at Arsenal in which he scored his first goal for the club, a stunning long-range volley.

'We were playing the cautious game – maybe play him in one game, then leave him out – but then he came on against Arsenal and changed the complexion of the game on that side of the field,' admitted Ferguson. 'He came on with an urgency to win the match for us. Every time the ball was on that side of the pitch, he was like a rat up a drainpipe. Everything seemed to happen at electric speed, and his tackling and urgency to get forward and play quickly ... he was absolutely outstanding. It was marvellous to see a young kid come on in a big game like that and he took it by the scruff of the neck, really. It goes a long way to convince you that the boy's ready for it all.'

The manager backed his assertion by fielding Rafael regularly in the pursuit of five major trophies, and the Brazilian ended the campaign with winners' medals from the Premier League and Club

World Cup, having also featured in each round of the League Cup before missing the final through injury. A nomination for the PFA's Young Player of the Year award served only to underline the staggering impact of his debut season.

Inevitably, however, for an 18-year-old learning his trade in a foreign environment, Rafael was a work in progress. His strengths were unquestionably his proactivity and commitment, but they could also prove detrimental in being caught out of position, sustaining knocks and strains and amassing cautions. The latter proved particularly costly a year on, as two bookings and a subsequent red card cost United control of a finely poised Champions League quarter-final against Bayern Munich.

'It was the worst experience I've had in all my life,' Rafa later confirmed, after United's away-goals exit. 'That night I learnt that in football you can go from heaven to hell in a matter of minutes. I was playing really well in the first half and then . . . well, you know what happened. If I hadn't have been sent off, we almost certainly would have won the match and my life would be much easier. It would have taken a lot of weight off my shoulders. I feel like I have to prove myself all over again and show everybody I'm capable of being a Manchester United player.'

His hopes of quickly doing so were hampered by regular injury setbacks, restricting his contribution to just 25 starts during the 2010-11 campaign. That was still ten more than the previous term, but Rafael had to endure the unusual situation of being usurped as United's first-choice right-back by his twin brother, culminating in Fabio starting the Champions League final against Barcelona. 'I'm happy for him,' Rafa insisted ahead of the game. 'He has had a tough start at United, but now he is showing how good he is and I will be cheering him on at Wembley.'

Though Pep Guardiola's unstoppable side overcame the Reds in London, the second Premier League title of Rafael's United career provided no small compensation. The following campaign, however, would carry less reward. The Brazilian dislocated his shoulder in training before the opening game of the 2011-12 season, immediately facing a ten-week spell on the sidelines.

'Being injured is the worst feeling in the world, but you can't let yourself get too down,' he said. 'You just have to work hard, come into the training ground every day and do the exercises you know will help you recover. Watching the games is the most difficult part, though. You're in the stands, but all you want to do is get out there and help.

'Some of my injuries, you just don't hear about people having them very often. I've dislocated my right shoulder twice and needed an operation to help it heal. It's not usual for footballers to injure shoulders – and for it to happen twice, I can only say it must be down to bad luck. Maybe it could be the way I play, but that's the way I am. I like to play with passion and when I'm on the pitch I can't worry about getting hurt or stop making tackles. I just want to play football and give my all.'

Restricted to just 15 starts in 2011-12, Rafa was largely a bystander in a thrilling title race with Manchester City, and was back on the sidelines watching on helplessly as City's two injury-time goals against Queens Park Rangers on the final day of the season wrenched the title across Manchester to leave everyone at Old Trafford devastated. 'The way we lost it hurt us so much,' he admitted. 'So badly that we knew we had to work so hard every game in the next season and not stop.' None worked harder than Rafael, who enjoyed by far his best campaign since moving to Old Trafford at a time of personal upheaval, becoming a father while Fabio joined QPR on loan for the entire 2012-13 campaign.

Free of injury, the bombarding right-back became a first-team fixture and was one of the stars of the campaign. 'I start every season hoping to make an impression and play a lot of games, but I couldn't have imagined how well this season has gone for me,' he said midway through his fifth season in England. 'I'm not a young player any more. I feel like I've developed and I want to play in every single game.

'I've waited a long time for this – getting to this point hasn't happened overnight. I've been at this club for five years, and that's a long time. At first, the goal was to just play one game for Manchester United. Then, when you achieve that, you set other targets. Now I want to play every game and become a regular in the team. I think this is just a natural development; it's bound to happen when you play more games and have more experiences. My daughter has also helped me – being a father has settled me down a lot. When you're a dad you have to be mature. Also, I think splitting from Fabio has been a good experience. At first I was sad, but I've come to see that it's made me grow up a lot. I've had to change and be more responsible.'

A more mature defender and also a more regular goalscorer, including two sensational goals at Liverpool and Queens Park Rangers, Rafa was one of the stars of a campaign which would yield United's 20th title and, moreover, would prove to be Sir Alex Ferguson's final season in management. 'You can't put his career into words,' said the defender. 'He was such a big influence on so many people and it was an honour to work with him.'

The Reds' struggles to cope in the immediate aftermath of Ferguson's departure made for a tough 2013-14 season for Rafael, with new manager David Moyes understandably open to trialling various players in the right-back role as he sought to weigh up his preferences. While Rafa was in and out of the reckoning under Moyes, he still featured often enough to notch 29 appearances, his second highest season since his arrival at the club. He also became his family's sole representative at the club after Fabio's sale to Cardiff City, but demonstrated enough of an upturn in form towards the end of Moyes's reign to suggest that he is ready to reclaim the right-back berth as his own.

A player quickly clutched to the bosom of United supporters,

Rafael is not only the embodiment of a modern full-back; he is a player flooded with the very ethos of the club, as an exponent of football as an expressive outlet and a tool of enjoyment.

3. LUKE SHAW

Position: Defender
Born: 12 July 1995; Kingston-upon-Thames, England
Previous club: Southampton
Joined United: 27 June 2014
Debut: 27 September 2014 vs West Ham United (H), Premier League
Honours: None

On 8 October 2012, in front of just 408 spectators at Moss Lane, home of Conference North side Altrincham FC, Luke Shaw lined up for Southampton's Under-21s ahead of an entertaining 3-3 draw with United. While his was an eye-catching performance that yielded a sumptuous assist from the left wing, nobody could have dreamt the trajectory that his fledgling career would follow.

Some 20 months later, having cemented a first-team place at Saints and appeared at the World Cup with England, Shaw joined the Louis van Gaal revolution as the most expensive teenager in football, moving to Old Trafford just a day after fellow new signing Ander Herrera. Not bad, considering he was yet to pass his driving test and had only just moved out of digs.

'It's really weird to think I was playing against the reserves two years ago and now I am signing for the club,' Luke admitted, just a few moments after scribbling his name across a lucrative four-year contract that would keep him at Old Trafford until at least 2018. 'It is obviously really good, but at Southampton we were taught to handle pressure and that is something I can deal with. Hopefully, I can keep doing what I am doing and improve. Who knows what is next for me, but I just want to improve my game and show the new gaffer what I can do.'

Of course, Shaw's meteoric rise has not been fuelled by luck or good fortune. It can be attributed to an incredible work ethic that was forged when passed from club to club as a child. Indeed, his first dalliance with a professional team came as an eight-year-old at Arsenal, whose decision to omit him from their academy squad prompted a switch to nearby Chelsea. While disappointed by the Gunners, this had appeared an idyllic move for a Blues supporter from Surrey whose dream was to play at Stamford Bridge.

However, dreams seldom come true and Shaw was soon turned away for being 'too small', a blow that led to another similarly fruitless spell at neighbouring Fulham. Unperturbed, despite a series of rejections, a six-week trial at Southampton proved successful and schoolboy forms were signed at St Mary's Stadium, beginning a pivotal relationship with the south coast club. 'I still remember the first day of my trial at Southampton,' Luke recalls. 'I got a phone call straight away to say they wanted to take me on. I couldn't believe it!'

As with most children trying to become professional footballers, Shaw owed a debt of gratitude to his parents, Paul and Joanna, who drove him down to Southampton's Staplewood training ground up to four times a week over a seven-year period. It was a gruelling journey that took an hour and 45 minutes each way, which was often extended by the frustrations of traffic. But, like every loving parent, they did it to give their son a chance of living his dream – not because he could be a star.

This grounded approach was maintained at Saints, where Shaw would steadily ascend a youth system that included fellow graduates Gareth Bale, Theo Walcott and Alex Oxlade-Chamberlain. While clearly a talented player, Luke was not exceptional until aged 15 when he moved into digs with a family in Southampton, a bold decision that quickly paid dividends. He became a regular for Jason Dodd's Under-18s and earned a first-team debut at 16 during an FA Cup third-round draw at Millwall. Although he watched from the stands for the remainder of that 2011-12 season, in which Nigel Adkins' men were promoted from the Championship, Shaw's chance to shine was approaching.

A first professional start duly arrived in a Capital One Cup win at Stevenage in August 2012, paving the way for his Premier League debut at West Brom three months later. By May, Shaw had clocked up 28 first-team appearances, which prompted Southampton to tie him down to a new five-year contract that would warn off potential suitors such as United and Chelsea. In completing this deal, the influence of new Argentine boss Mauricio Pochettino was clear. 'The manager has done a lot for me, especially for my fitness, and this year is going to be a big year for me,' Shaw explained at the time. 'I've come back very, very fit and better than last season, so I can't wait for the new season to get started.'

Bigger, fitter and more experienced, Shaw continued to excel throughout the 2013-14 campaign and registered another 41 first-team outings, impressively missing just three top-flight games as Saints became the league's surprise package by securing an eighth-place finish – sitting just eight points behind David Moyes's United. Having caught the eye, a first England cap was earned in March 2014, stepping off the bench as a half-time replacement for Chelsea's Ashley Cole during a 1-0 friendly win over Denmark.

Club team-mate Rickie Lambert was an unused substitute that night and, given that the latter spent years climbing the Football League with no less than five clubs before eventually hitting the big time at Southampton, their roads to international stardom were of contrasting lengths. But as the 32-year-old former beetroot factory worker and new Liverpool striker explained, he could not have been happier for his teenage friend. 'Luke must think it is this easy for everyone, but it shows just how well he has done and he deserves everything he is getting,' Lambert told reporters. 'To be where he is in such short time is unbelievable. He has everything and not many people get past him. The best wingers in the Premier League won't get the better of him. I can't remember one. For such a young lad it is frightening, really.'

Indeed, as Lambert pointed out, a host of big names struggled to make an impact against Shaw's defensive quality and even our very own Adnan Januzaj was shackled during the final match of the season, which saw United and Southampton play out a meaning-less 1-1 draw at St Mary's with league positions already confirmed. Luke was just as potent going forward that day and one marauding run that left Chris Smalling trailing in his wake looked as though a point was being made to both England and United. The game was also notable for its finale, which saw Shaw and his Liverpool-bound team-mate Adam Lallana exit the action to heroes' ovations from an appreciative home crowd, which was all too aware of what the summer might hold for their star players.

During the 2013-14 season, as reward for an excellent campaign, Shaw was named in the PFA's Team of the Year and was also one of six nominees for their Young Player of the Year award that was even-tually won by Chelsea playmaker Eden Hazard. Nevertheless, the most significant individual honour was provided by Hodgson, who took the brave but logical decision to include the international rookie in his 23-man World Cup squad as cover for Everton's Leighton Baines. 'I was very surprised,' Luke admitted. 'With Ashley Cole not playing many games, I thought I may be in with a chance. But he played the last three games in the season and he played incredibly well. It made me think that maybe this is not my time, but obviously I saw I was announced in the squad and it was the best feeling in the world. I was sitting there with my family and friends and we were just all so proud that I'm only eighteen and involved in a World Cup.'

Having watched from the bench as England suffered consecutive 2-1 defeats to Italy and Uruguay, losses which meant the Three Lions could no longer reach the knockout rounds, Shaw became the youngest player at the 2014 competition by starting the goalless draw with group winners Costa Rica, playing a full match and keeping a clean sheet alongside United's Phil Jones and Chris Smalling. While this stalemate was hardly the glorious climax the nation dreamt of, it meant everything to a certain teenager from Kingston-upon-Thames, whose summer was about to get even better.

On 27 June, just two days after returning home from Brazil, Shaw concluded his much-rumoured transfer to United and cut a relieved figure while completing a medical at the Aon Training Complex. 'It's a great feeling,' he explained. 'I've known for a number of weeks that United were interested in me. I was hoping it might have been done before the World Cup but it wasn't and now I'm finally here, getting it done. I'm very pleased. Manchester United is the biggest club in the world and is always going to be up there with the best. I think the main reason I've come here is because United want to win trophies and so do I. As a young lad, I aspired to win trophies. I can't wait to start!'

Upon completing the deal and understandably keen to impress, Shaw cut short his already brief holiday to report early for training. As you might expect, news of his transfer to United was met with great excitement and enthusiasm by Reds supporters, feelings that were only enhanced by Gary Neville's ringing endorsement of the deal. 'I am trying to keep guarded here about the size of talent that exists in this footballer,' the club legend and England coach praised. 'You are talking about brilliant potential. The reason United spent so much money on a left-back at his age is because they see the huge talent and I can only endorse that talent. You have to watch him at close hand to realise that this is an incredible and hugely talented football player. Luke Shaw is fantastic.

'United fans have got to understand – and this is not the boy's fault – that when you sign someone at that age, you don't get perfection straight away, but you have to give him time and space to develop. Luke will need time to settle in, as any nineteen-year-old boy would coming to Manchester United. I am expecting he will do well this season, but you will see a quite fantastic full-back in eighteen months to two years. When he matures and gets used to the club, settles into the environment and understands the expectation then he will blossom.

'I came through at sixteen to seventeen years of age with the rest of my mates and we virtually lived in the football club. We knew the expectations. It was drilled into us. He is coming from a very good football club and a very good youth system but he is now at a giant of a club. The expectations are massive, but he will get used to that. I am hoping that, from a football point of view, he is allowed to develop. The manager he has now got in Louis van Gaal has a track record of working with young players, so it is all perfect for Luke. He has joined absolutely the right football club in terms of his development. He can achieve anything he wants at Manchester United.'

Given that Shaw's career has already progressed at breakneck speed, progressing from Moss Lane to Old Trafford in just two years, only a fool would bet against him realising his dreams in the Theatre that nurtures them.

4. PHIL JONES

Position: Defender
Born: 21 February 1992; Preston, England
Previous club: Blackburn Rovers
Joined United: 1 July 2011
Debut: 7 August 2011 vs Manchester City (N), Community Shield
Honours: Premier League (2012-13), Community Shield (2011, 2013)

Saturday, 27 November 2010. All around the celebrating Nani and his joyous team-mates, Old Trafford was reverberating with blood-lust, sensing a victory of legendary margins over a Blackburn Rovers team which had just shipped two goals in a minute, Nani's being the fifth in 48 minutes for a rampant United side. Sir Alex Ferguson was not focused entirely on his side's staggering display, however; it was a blue-and-white-clad figure who had caught his eye.

Phil Jones, aged just 18 but performing manfully while those around him crumbled, was lambasting his senior peers and urging them to salvage at least some modicum of pride from a situation of searing embarrassment. 'When they lost the fifth goal, he was the one out there giving them all stick. That impressed me,' Ferguson later admitted. 'I was convinced we had to get him.'

The Scot's gut feeling has been validated in the ensuing seasons. Now in his fourth term at Old Trafford, Jones has demonstrated that fighting spirit ever since his 2011 move from Ewood Park. It should come as little surprise, according to Phil Hindley, Jones's manager during his time as a nine-year-old in Ribble Wanderers' Under-10s team. 'He was a winner, even as a kid,' said Hindley. 'Even in the five-a-side game at the end of training, Phil was desperate to win. He absolutely hated losing. He had great will to win and strength of character.

'What particularly struck me about him at the time was his physical strength. A year's age gap at that stage is quite significant, but he more than held his own. His resistance to physical pain was exceptional as well. At that age, they'll go flying into a tackle, run on for a bit and then require treatment and there would be tears. With Phil you could see he was physically very strong and had a very high pain threshold, too.

'He's the best header of a ball I've seen among kids, even at that age. At nine he could make that classic jump where the player seems to almost hover, and I remember him winning a cup final for us with one such header from a corner. You can still see that power and desire in him now. He's obviously a long way away from the lad who I worked with, but there are still traits that I recognise.'

Brave, bullish and powerful, Jones has retained his core strengths throughout his evolution as a footballer. It was with Ribble that he first came to Blackburn's attention, and after featuring in a variety of positions for Rovers' much-vaunted youth team under coach Gary Bowyer, he gained international recognition at just 17 years of age. Problem was, an errant assumption of his ineligibility almost denied him a chance of representing England.

'With a name like that, I had just assumed that he was Welsh,' laughed Noel Blake, England's Under-19s coach. 'I was aware of Phil from my time at Stoke, when he impressed against us for Blackburn. When I went to the national team, I went into Blackburn to do some work with Gary Bowyer, who was then their Academy coach. Phil walked past and I said: "I've always liked him; shame he's Welsh." "No, he's English," Gary said. Phil came into the next squad.

'He had always played well at the back for Blackburn, and that's where he came in for us for his debut, and for the opening game in our European Championship qualifiers alongside Steven Caulker, but after that his final two games for us were both in a midfield holding role next to [former United midfielder] Matty James. He was outstanding. His team game and understanding were terrific, and his ability to get forward as well was an important factor.

'He wasn't just a holding player who sat there all day long. He had – and has – the intelligence to know when and where to get forward. He did it from central defence, too. In a really tight game against Republic of Ireland, Phil stepped out from the back and drove from the edge of our box to the edge of their box and got a foul. We scored from the resulting free-kick and won the game one-nil, so he made the difference from that position.'

Jones was fast outgrowing junior football, and he was able to demonstrate his gameness at first-team level when Rovers manager Sam Allardyce opted to hand the 18-year-old his Premier League bow against title-chasing Chelsea in March 2010. Up against Blues behemoth Didier Drogba, Jones was unfazed and went on to win the Man-of-the-Match award in a 1-1 draw, leaving the field draped in John Terry's shirt. At one point during the game, he thundered into consecutive 50-50 challenges with both Drogba and Frank Lampard, emerging with the ball on both occasions and sending the Ewood Park crowd wild.

Later that month, United sampled his teak-tough approach, and could only register a damaging goalless draw at Ewood. Jones once again shone, and took home the Man-of-the-Match award. He would stay with Rovers for one more season, in which his drive and talent earned him a string of admirers, but it was the lure of United which tempted him away from Blackburn in the summer of 2011.

Though ostensibly recruited as a central defender, Jones began his United career in versatile fashion, also spending time as a marauding right-back and a holding midfielder. His stint at full-back in the Reds' breakneck opening to the 2011-12 season led to several goals, while his no-nonsense tackling and breathless omnipresence made him an invaluable option in the midfield minefield. 'He's very versatile,' observed Ferguson. 'He's mobile, he's determined and it gives us options.'

According to Hindley, Jones's youth team manager, such adaptability was nothing new. 'Phil never even played in the back four for us,' he said. 'You could play him anywhere across the midfield or anywhere upfront and he'd regularly be among our top scorers. It's definitely rare to see a kid with the football intelligence to do that at that age. One or two positions, maybe, but not that many, and especially not when they're playing with kids a year older than them like Phil was.'

Jones's first campaign with the Reds was spread across all three positions and, despite yielding a clutch of exciting displays, there would be no happy ending. Mere seconds away from picking up his first Premier League winner's medal on the final day of the season after winning at Sunderland, Phil watched on agog as news filtered through to the Stadium of Light that Manchester City had pinched the title with almost the last kick of the season.

Retribution wouldn't be long in coming for United but, for Jones, there were twists and turns throughout the following season as he suffered a succession of injuries. A knee operation ruled him out for almost the first half of the campaign, and less than three months later he sustained ankle damage against Reading which cost him a place in the side against Real Madrid in what would prove to be Sir Alex Ferguson's final Champions League outing. Yet, the youngster still ended the campaign on a high, picking up his first league title and earning staggeringly high praise from Ferguson, who said: 'Arguably, the way he is looking, he could be our best ever player.'

Praise has poured forth for Jones throughout his short career to date. Likened to United great Duncan Edwards by Sir Bobby Charlton, he also draws positive comparisons outside Old Trafford. 'Jones is a talent,' said former England manager, Fabio Capello. 'Young, but a big talent because when he receives the ball he plays always without fear. Good passes, good solutions. I know something about football and the solution that he chooses every time when he receives the ball is always the best. It is difficult to find a player like him, really difficult. He can play in different positions always at the top level. I found in my career probably two players like that – Franco Baresi and Fernando Hierro. They played as midfielders and after they played centre-back. They were really good players!'

After the shock retirement of Ferguson, David Moyes sought to use Jones primarily as a centre-back, but soon succumbed to the temptation to have him plug gaps elsewhere in the team, with his versatility most apparent in an important victory over league leaders Arsenal. Deployed initially in a midfield holding role, Jones moved to central defence after 45 minutes to compensate for Nemanja Vidic's withdrawal with injury. Outstanding displays in both roles, in a game of such high stakes, served only to underline his talent.

'People keep going on that Phil needs to find a position,' said then first-team coach Phil Neville, himself a versatile operator in a variety of defensive and midfield roles during his playing career. 'I don't worry about that because eventually he will find his position. People forget how young he is. If he's a centre-back, centre-backs don't peak until they're twenty-seven, twenty-eight or twenty-nine. Look back on Rio Ferdinand, who has been one of the very best centre-backs. Early in his career he played in a three, sometimes as a sweeper, the odd game in midfield, and then when he got to twenty-six he was a centre-back and he was one of the best centre-backs. That's what it's going to be like for Phil.

'He's going to be great in midfield in some games, great at centre-back in some games, but what he has got is the physical capacity to play in every position on the pitch, so that's a massive strength and he shouldn't worry about nailing down a position. I've seen him play for England in midfield, at right-back and at centre-back and he could be the best in that position in the country, so he just needs to keep progressing the way he's doing.

'As long as he listens and keeps learning, Joner can be as good as he wants to be. Phil's got all the natural ability needed to play in any position on the pitch. Now the concentration part comes. That comes with age and experience. Cut out mistakes; if the ball's being cleared, clear it properly, get in the right positions. There will come a time when he has to start leading that back four, start being the Steve Bruce, the Jaap Stam, the Rio Ferdinand and lead the back four, bring people into position, because he is a leader in the way that he plays. People feed off his enthusiasm and he leads the team.'

The 2014-15 campaign sees Jones working under the tutelage of Louis van Gaal and quickly brought further change: the introduction of a three-man central defence flanked by wing-backs. Typically, the England international was keen to embrace the challenge. 'I personally enjoy the system,' said Jones. 'When everyone is working well together and knows what they should be doing on the pitch, then it certainly works and is very difficult for teams to play against. I think the more we train and play the more people understand their role on the pitch.'

Ironically, despite van Gaal's famed penchant for versatile players, Jones appears to have now pinned down his favoured position in central defence. Be it in a back three or a reversion to a back four, time will tell, but in times of ongoing change at United, it seems certain that Phil Jones will be a central figure to the Reds' evolution.

5. MARCOS ROJO

Position: Defender
Born: 20 March 1990; La Plata, Argentina
Previous clubs: Estudiantes, Spartak Moscow, Sporting Lisbon
Joined United: 20 August 2014
Debut: 14 September 2014 vs Queens Park Rangers (H), Premier League
Honours: None

Fast, forceful and fierce, Marcos Rojo fits the stereotype of a teak-tough Argentinian defender, and the 24-year-old arrived in England in the summer of 2014 to reinforce United's defence with his grit and physicality.

Less than a month after helping oust Louis van Gaal's Netherlands squad from the 2014 World Cup semi-final, Rojo found himself reunited with the Dutchman. The defender's displays in Brazil were of sufficient quality to warrant his inclusion as the only Argentinian in the team of the tournament, and van Gaal was among those struck by his form.

'I played him in the World Cup against Argentina, so I had to analyse Argentina,' said the United manager. 'From that video I was already enchanted about him because my philosophy is you have to buy players who fit in the profile, and I think Marcos fits in the profile as a left central defender but also as a left wing-back. He played a fantastic World Cup, so I am very pleased.'

After a lengthy wait to be granted a work permit wound to a happy ending, Rojo expressed his delight. 'I am desperate to get onto the field and play, because I have not been able to,' he said. 'My life has changed a lot. I am very happy to be at Manchester United, a top team in the world, sharing a dressing room with players like Wayne Rooney, Robin van Persie, Angel Di Maria and Radamel Falcao. Everything that has happened to me since the World Cup has been a dream. This is a very important step in my career as a player and as a person.'

Marcos's first steps in professional football were taken with Estudiantes in La Plata, where he graduated to senior football at the age of 19 and played alongside former United record signing Juan Sebastian Veron. Rojo was part of the Estudiantes squad which ruled South America by winning the Copa Libertadores and almost shocked Barcelona in the Club World Cup final, and he had established himself as a first-team fixture by the time of the club's Argentinian Primera Division triumph of 2010.

His exciting performances boasted lightning speed, unyielding commitment and occasionally spectacular goals, so it was little surprise when European clubs began to take notice of him. It was Spartak Moscow who moved to the front of the queue, snapping up the 20-year-old in December 2010, but his time in Russia proved a short-lived yet taxing affair.

'When he signed from Estudiantes, he was just a champion and was a promising full-back at twenty years of age,' said Ivan Kalashnikov, editor-in-chief of Sports.ru. 'He was not considered a major signing and he was still very young, but it just didn't work out for him at all.

He was a left-back but Spartak needed a centre-back more, so he was quickly moved and wasn't given much time to adapt to Russian football. He was quickly converted and played at centre-back.

'The problem at Spartak was that it was a very unstable club – a shambles at times – and he was always with various different centre-backs and he didn't really form a partnership in central defence. They had something like ten central defensive partnerships in 2011-12, so he never really had a chance to settle. He needed to adapt more quickly than he expected, probably, while being moved positionally which I don't think helped. It just wasn't the club to be at. He didn't even get to go forward for corners to show that he could score; instead, he had to wait on the halfway line as cover against counter-attacks. Definitely he wasn't at the right place at the right time, and the bad spell at Spartak didn't convince anyone that Rojo was a bad player.'

Throughout his turbulent time with Spartak, Rojo retained the faith of Alejandro Sabella, his former Estudiantes manager, who had taken the reins of Argentina's national team and continued to call on his former charge, despite the youngster's club issues. He was also still being keenly monitored by other clubs, and Sporting Lisbon signed him in the summer of 2012. Yet, despite finding an escape route from his Russian nightmare, the defender was unable to locate his best form upon relocating to Portugal.

'Spartak were happy to sell him, and his first season in Lisbon did not go much better,' said Tom Kundert, editor of Portugoal.net. 'Sporting had a terrible campaign, finishing seventh, and he was a liability at centre-back, although he performed better at left-back when he was occasionally used there. It took time, and curiously, he had a similar time in Portugal as the other centre-back who went from Portugal to Manchester in 2014, Eliaquim Mangala, who joined Manchester City. Both were raw and reckless to start with.'

In the 2013-14 season, that all changed for Rojo, who shone and emerged as the leader of a frugal defence as Sporting returned to character and finished second in the league. 'It was remarkable to see such a transformation in a player from one season to the next,' said Kundert. 'If you had suggested in 2013 that Manchester United would pay big money for him, nobody would have believed it, but not now, after his performances last term and in the World Cup. I'm struggling to think of any other player who improved so much from one season to the next. It really was night and day. His ability to learn from his mistakes augurs well for his future career.'

By the time of his departure from Portugal, Rojo had evolved into a proactive, forceful behemoth in the heart of the Sporting defence. His aerial dominance at both ends of the field marked him out against most opponents, while his searing pace provided an invaluable ace up the sleeve whenever required. It was no surprise when Marcos was named in Argentina's squad for the World Cup, but his exploits in Brazil unquestionably raised eyebrows. His first international goal secured a final group-stage win over Nigeria, but it was his all-action exploits in a well-drilled Argentinian defence which most impressed.

Though disappointed to see his country fall to Germany in extra time of the final, Atlético Madrid coach Diego Simeone singled out the youngster for special praise: 'Rojo won the hearts of the Argentines at the World Cup,' he said. 'He was very good, both attacking and defending. Sabella put his trust in him and he responded really well. He had an excellent World Cup and was the best left-back among the four semi-finalists.'

A place in the tournament's all-star team wasn't the only reward for Rojo's excellence. When Louis van Gaal sought to replace the experienced but departed Nemanja Vidic and Rio Ferdinand, the Argentine proved to be the outstanding solution. The prospect of moving to a third country in four years was a daunting one, but Rojo consulted a former team-mate who knew all about life in the Premier League with United. 'Before agreeing to sign for Manchester, I spoke a lot with Veron and he suggested a few things to me,' Marcos revealed.

Though his capture from Sporting was far from a straightforward affair, with issues surrounding the player's ownership and later difficulties securing a work permit, Rojo completed his move in August 2014 and he made no secret of what he planned to bring to Old Trafford.

'It's taken a while for everything to get sorted out because these transfers can be very difficult, but I'm so happy to be here at Manchester United,' he said, upon his arrival in England. 'It's amazing to be joining the biggest club in the world. I always follow the Premier League, and Manchester United were always my team because they were the biggest and the best. Juan Sebastian Veron played for United and was a great player and I always watched his progress. United were always my club.

'I think the most important thing is that I keep growing as a player and keep improving. I have worked really hard for this opportunity and now I am at the biggest club in the world and I want to win trophies. I always give everything I have in a game and I leave everything out there on the pitch. I play each game as if it could be my last. That's the most important thing in my philosophy.'

The Argentinian's no-nonsense, full-blooded style of defending has inevitably led to disciplinary issues throughout his career, at each club and also at the World Cup, where he missed his country's quarter-final victory after picking up two bookings in three group games. Adapting his style sympathetically to a new foreign league is something which his manager was mindful of, even before he had kicked a ball for the Reds.

'He has to be aggressive in the right moment and when I have to say something – or criticise – maybe that's it,' said van Gaal. 'He has to control himself in every moment. That might be something he needs to improve and I hope I can help him. First of all, he needs a lot of brains, to be aware of spaces, because we are defending spaces and that's the first word I used to him. He also has to be a very good header, because the Premier League is also always playing with long balls and also his build has to be good. I liked the way he played in the World Cup. That's also very important, the [physical] build-up qualities.'

A major factor in Rojo's identification was his versatility. The marauding left-back was forced to add a new dimension to his game during spells in the centre of the Spartak Moscow and Sporting Lisbon defences, and his ability to perform either role sits well with van Gaal, whose penchant for trialling different formations was underlined by his use of a three-man central defence with wing-backs upon arriving at United.

With Rojo able to function in four roles – left-back, left wing-back or on the left side of either a two- or three-man central defence – his adaptability appealed hugely to his manager. 'It is my philosophy to only buy players who fit the profile, and I think Marcos fits the profile as a left-sided central defender, as well as a left wing-back,' said the Dutchman. 'He played as a left wing-back for Argentina at the World Cup, but as a centre-back at Sporting Lisbon. He was fantastic at the World Cup so I'm very pleased.'

United's only previous Argentinian defender was Gabriel Heinze, who arrived with a similar reputation and quickly forced his way into favouritism with supporters through his unyielding commitment to the cause. The Old Trafford crowd has always had a soft spot for a hard man and, in Marcos Rojo, there is now another robust Argentinian for fans to admire.

6. JONNY EVANS

Position: Defender
Born: 3 January 1988; Belfast, Northern Ireland
Previous clubs: Royal Antwerp, Sunderland (both loans)
Joined United: 1 July 2004
Debut: 26 September 2007 vs Coventry City (H), League Cup

Honours: Premier League (2008-09, 2010-11, 2012-13), FIFA Club World Cup (2008), League Cup (2008-09, 2009-10), Community Shield (2008, 2010, 2011, 2013)

For all the fame and financial reward on offer to modern footballers, some realise different dreams by enjoying the undiluted romance of playing for their own boyhood club. Such a dream came true for life-long Manchester United supporter Jonny Evans.

The Northern Irishman – who was born in Belfast, the city of George Best – has a genuine love for the Reds and carries a humble appreciation for the privileged position he has found himself in. There is nothing flash about him and he is certainly not wasteful with his money, 'because my parents always encouraged me not to be'.

'My first recollections of Manchester United would be going way back, probably to my granny's house and having these little figures of various players,' Jonny explained. 'Even before that, I got a United poster for Christmas when I was five years old. My bedroom was all done out in Manchester United stuff: bed covers, posters, the lot. So it goes back to when I was just a kid.

'It's hard to put into words exactly what Manchester United means to me. From a young age, I was fanatical about United and I used to cry when the team lost. That's how much it meant as a kid. Now I feel really privileged to pull on the shirt and go out there and try to make a difference and represent the fans on the pitch.'

Evans was raised in the tough Rathcoole estate where Reds legend Norman Whiteside also earned his stripes. It is also where mother and father, Dawn and Jackie, kept a tight family unit that included younger siblings Katie and former academy graduate Corry, who left United for Hull City in 2011 and is currently on the books at Blackburn Rovers in the Championship.

His dad had played for Chelsea and Arsenal as a youngster but failed to make the first team, an experience that yielded educational benefits for him when clubs were first interested in his eldest. 'Joining the club actually happened over a number of years,' Jonny recalls. 'When I was nine years old, a scout had come over to watch me play in Northern Ireland and asked me if I wanted to join the Manchester United centre of excellence. For me that was a massive thing.

'I was fortunate in that my dad had been at Chelsea when he was younger. He'd moved to London when he was sixteen, so he'd gone through that process and knew that I was still a bit away, even though I was only nine and I was getting really excited. He was telling me that there's still so much to go.

'Then when I was maybe ten, I made my first trip to Manchester. I then travelled over on every school holiday and it was great at the time. When you first go to the stadium it's like a dream. I'd never actually been across to Old Trafford as a young kid, even though I was a Manchester United fanatic. My mum and dad had never managed to get across to take me to a game, so it wasn't until I got a trial. The club took me and a few players to see a game.

'It was a great experience and even though I knew I had a long way to go before I could play at Old Trafford myself, it definitely gave me the inspiration to want to play there one day. I moved across with my whole family when I was fifteen, and I think that was really the start of it all, when I moved to England. It's been over eleven years now, it's been a long experience but it feels like yesterday.'

Having ascended the Academy ranks, Evans spent the first half of the 2006-07 season on loan at Belgian club Royal Antwerp before temporarily moving to Sunderland in December to play under his boyhood hero Roy Keane. The Black Cats comfortably earned promotion to the Premier League that term, with Jonny also winning the club's Youth Player of the Year award to cap an enlightening experience at the Stadium of Light.

'Roy Keane was always my favourite player growing up as a young United fan, like he was for a lot of Irish fans,' said Jonny. 'I first met him at Carrington on the exercise bikes in the gym. He came in one day and sat on the bike next to me. He asked what my name was and how it was going, and then introduced himself as Roy. I was like, "I know exactly who you are – you're Roy Keane!" It was great to meet him and then work together at Sunderland. I really enjoyed it.'

Playing with added experience and defensive guile, the Northern Irishman eventually made his United debut during a 2-0 League Cup defeat to Coventry City in September 2007. He then rejoined Sunderland at the turn of the New Year to help them successfully retain their top-flight status, as Keane's men finished three points above the relegation zone in 15th place. With his short-term mission accomplished, Jonny was ready to challenge for the first team at Old Trafford.

'I loved my time at Sunderland,' he admitted shortly afterwards. 'In my first season there we won the Championship with Roy Keane as manager, and the next season I went back and managed to stay in the Premier League, which was another good achievement. It gave me a good platform to return to United and fight for a first-team spot.'

After returning from Wearside, Evans featured in every one of United's 2008-09 pre-season games as his status grew in the eyes of Sir Alex Ferguson. Sure enough, he became the contingency plan for whenever the rock-solid partnership of Rio Ferdinand and Nemanja Vidic broke up, filling the breach in every competition that campaign. Importantly, he finished the term with a hat-trick of winners' medals from the FIFA Club World Cup, the League Cup and the Premier League.

Another 28 outings were registered in 2009-10, before making 21 more in 2010-11 en route to his second domestic crown. While a valuable squad asset at this point, it was not until the following season that Evans really came into own. Spurred on by the arrival of Chris Smalling and Phil Jones, two fledgling centre-backs, the Belfast boy stepped up his game and brilliantly filled the void left by Nemanja Vidic, who had damaged major ligaments in his knee during a Champions League defeat at FC Basel in December. As Sir Alex observed, Jonny required the challenge at this stage of his career and went on to play 40 games that season – his best total yet as a United player.

'Evans, I think, needed a shake,' Ferguson wrote in his most recent autobiography. 'He didn't appreciate me signing Jones and Smalling. It caused him to question my opinion of him. But he proved himself in his own right and did increasingly well for us. It's always gratifying when a player responds to new arrivals by redoubling his efforts.' The former manager went on to describe the Academy graduate as 'arguably the best defender in the country', a compliment that was fully deserved.

With his confidence at an all-time high, Jonny produced his most impressive form during Sir Alex's final season as manager, when a 20th English league title was won in sensational fashion. He even discovered his scoring boots that year, finding the net on four separate occasions. As he admitted, it was fairytale stuff for the man whose dreams all centred on playing for his beloved Manchester United.

'When you look back at the players who have represented Manchester United, some great players, it drives you to want to be mentioned in the same bracket,' he commented. 'Also, being part of a good team helps. I grew up watching the teams that Sir Alex Ferguson built over the years, so to be a part of that was a great feeling. It's also about winning trophies because that is ultimately what goes down in history.'

While a blend of injury and competition for places limited Evans to just 25 appearances during the short-lived David Moyes era, he subsequently emerged as a prominent figure under Louis van Gaal. Although the attention of the sporting world is on Old Trafford in 2014-15, with widespread curiosity over how the club responds to finishing seventh in the league, Jonny says the biggest pressure stems from the crest on his chest.

'You feel the responsibility of playing for Manchester United every time you pull on the shirt,' he insisted. 'It's kind of strange because you grow up a fan but as soon as you become a player you kind of feel on the other side of it. You are representing the club on the pitch; you're still a fan but it's from a totally different perspective. You've got to try to make the fans happy as well as the manager and do your job for the club. As a footballer, though, the day you retire, I think you go back to being a fan like everyone else.'

With starting places up for grabs following the departures of defensive stalwarts Rio Ferdinand and Nemanja Vidic, Evans believes 2014-15 is perhaps the most important season of his Reds career. Now married and father to a newborn baby, the maturing 26-year-old is confident of hitting top form during his peak years at Old Trafford.

'If you look at Nemanja, he did not join us until he was twenty-five or twenty-six. I think I have benefited playing with Rio and Nemanja for a long time – and Wes Brown before that,' says Evans. 'I've learned a lot through my career. It is a big time for me now. I had an injury last pre-season and missed maybe the first month of the campaign. But once I got in and played, I got on a pretty good run. That was the strongest period and I felt really good, even though the results weren't coming. I wasn't playing the way that I wanted to play in the team, in terms of getting results, but I felt good physically.'

Jonny is keen to extend his stay in M16 and hopes to replicate the careers of former team-mates Gary Neville, Paul Scholes and Ryan Giggs, all one-club men whose names are all listed in the pantheon of Old Trafford legends. Having achieved so many of his boyhood dreams already, the lifelong Red has eyes on his next big ambition.

'I'd like to be a one-club man,' Evans said. 'Obviously I've had my loan spells but I've come through the Academy here and now I'm in the first team. When I was younger, clubs were asking me to go on trial from the age of ten or thirteen. I never went on trial at another club. I knew that Manchester United was the place I wanted to play football. So to play here throughout my career would be something I would look to do and I'd love to do it. But I can't look too far ahead. I'm still young, so I'll see where this takes me.'

7. ANGEL DI MARIA

Position: Winger
Born: 14 February 1988; Rosario, Argentina
Previous clubs: Rosario Central, Benfica, Real Madrid
Joined United: 26 August 2014
Debut: 30 August 2014 vs Burnley (A), Premier League
Honours: None

While some eyebrows were cocked by the enormous £59.7 million fee with which United parted to secure the services of Angel Di Maria, far more were raised by the Argentinian's early displays in the Reds' famous No.7 shirt.

Sporadic glimpses of the 26-year-old's brilliance were evident in his debut, a goalless draw at Burnley, but a thrilling home bow against Queens Park Rangers, which yielded a goal and two assists, prompted new team-mate Ander Herrera to gush: 'Angel is one of the best players in the world. Manchester United always has to have top players and he is one of the best.' Fellow Spaniard Juan Mata, meanwhile, opined: 'It seems he's been with us for a long time. Angel is a very enthusiastic guy, a great signing.'

The most expensive player in the history of British football went on to score another sublime goal in his next outing, lofting home an impish strike in the Reds' shock 3-5 defeat at Leicester City, to provide further cause for excitement at having one of the world's most exciting talents on the books at Old Trafford.

One of history's most expensive players has come a long way since his first tentative steps in football. 'My mother got tired of me breaking everything in the house so she took me to see a doctor when I was three,' he recalled. 'I was running around the examination room breaking everything. The doctor just said: "Sign him up for a sport" and that is where my career began.' By the age of four, Angel was registered with local side Torito in his native Perdriel, yet he was soon scouted by Rosario Central, the local top-flight club, and found himself at the centre of unlikely negotiations which culminated in Torito demanding – and receiving – a transfer fee of 35 footballs.

While it provided Di Maria's big break, there was no instant glamour for the energetic youngster, who later started working in coal mines with his family at the age of ten. Before then, however, he depended on his parents' sacrifice. His mother, Diana, would take him to each training session. 'She took me on a bicycle, three of us on that bike,' Angel recalled. 'I would sit on the back and my younger sister would sit on a seat on the handlebars and my mother would ride the bike. It was hard during winter!'

Nonetheless, the collective endeavour paid off as Di Maria gradually ascended into the first team, where just two years of senior football showcased enough of his talent to prompt interest from Portuguese giants Benfica. 'My father made so many sacrifices for me – I will always remember what he said when Benfica made a bid for me: "Son, this train only passes by once in a lifetime, so you have to get on and go forward,"' recalled Angel. 'I was heartbroken for my father, because he could have played football but got a serious knee injury playing for River Plate reserves. My mother always reminds me how lucky I am and that I am doing what my father wanted to do, I am living his dream. I feel blessed that I am now in a position to repay him and my family and make sure they don't have to struggle. My father worked at that coal yard for sixteen years until I made him give up work when I joined Benfica. It was nice to be in a position to be able to do that and say: "Dad, you don't have to do this any more."'

The slender, speedy starlet moved to Portugal shortly after starring in his country's success at the FIFA Under-20 World Cup, and his displays soon prompted senior international recognition. A gold medal at the 2008 Olympics preceded two Portuguese League Cup winners' medals, before Angel starred in Benfica's Primeira Liga success of 2009-10 during what proved to be his final campaign in Portugal. His displays prompted a move to Real Madrid as the first signing of Jose Mourinho's time at the Estadio Santiago Bernabeu, and there would be no let-up in the Argentinian's relentless improvement.

He crammed six major honours into four years in Spain, but it was during his three years working under the Portuguese that Di Maria blossomed into a world-class talent in a variety of positions. 'Mourinho made me a better player,' he admitted. 'He showed me many things and made me grow as a footballer. He helped me to move into a different position, to sacrifice myself more for the team. I'm very grateful to him. He told me that, at Real, I was a forward that could also defend and that I couldn't rest when they were on the attack. As I was performing under him for the three years he was at Madrid, he put me in the starting line-up. The Di Maria playing down the middle compared to the one now is a different player, both technically and tactically.'

Mourinho identified that Di Maria's talents were transferable from the left flank to almost anywhere across a front six. 'With space he is dangerous; even without it he can find a way to go one-on-one,' said the Portuguese. Di Maria's devastating pace, intelligence and moxie were just as incisive whether attacking from deeper positions or further up the field, and he starred in Real's Copa del Rey success of 2011 and their La Liga triumph of 2011-12. The departure of Mourinho in the summer of 2013 prompted the appointment of Carlo Ancelotti, and the Italian swiftly shattered the world transfer record to take Tottenham's Gareth Bale to Madrid. The ramifications for Di Maria were substantial.

'With Bale's arrival at the Santiago Bernabeu he had to convert into a midfielder,' said Spanish journalist Guillem Balague. 'He added something to Real Madrid. They've got very good positional midfielders, but he was the only one that who could break the lines of pressure from midfield and could jump from being a midfielder to being a forward. And he can be dangerous in the process, scoring goals from midfield, too.'

It was as a provider that Di Maria's evolution was at its starkest. No player supplied more assists during the 2013-14 Spanish league campaign, and it was he who allowed Real to decisively overcome Atlético Madrid in the Champions League final, breaking through Diego Simeone's side to prompt Bale's extra-time strike to set Los Blancos on their way to a record-extending tenth title. The Argentinian was presented with the Man-of-the-Match award by Sir Alex Ferguson afterwards, but few could have foreseen that the two would be reunited at Old Trafford a matter of months later.

In the interim, Di Maria shone on the biggest stage once again, excelling in Argentina's run to the World Cup final, even if he was cruelly deprived of the chance to feature in the semi-final and final by injury. Despite missing the last two games, Angel was named on the ten-man shortlist for FIFA's Golden Ball award for the tournament's best player. So too was James Rodriguez, and it was the Colombian's subsequent move to Madrid which convinced Di Maria that the time was right to seek out a new challenge.

Time remained for the Argentinian to win the UEFA Super Cup with Real, but his role as an unused substitute spoke volumes for what the future held. When he was also absent from the starting line-up in the subsequent meeting between Ancelotti's side and Atlético Madrid in the Supercoppa de Espana, Atleti manager Simeone was quick to revel in Real leaving out 'their best player'. The former Argentina star continued: 'He is the one that breaks through the opposition, tilting the balance of the game, and he makes the other players perform better.'

It appeared that appreciation for Di Maria was forthcoming from every angle, except from the powers-that-be at Real. 'Whether van Gaal is going to play with wide players, I'm not too sure, but whether it is the right- or left-hand side, Di Maria's pace is frightening,' commented club legend Paul Scholes. 'He can go past players and score goals. That is something we have been missing.'

On the day of the Reds' Capital One Cup mauling at MK Dons, the British record transfer was confirmed, also shattering the club record fee paid out for Juan Mata just seven months earlier. Back in Madrid, the discontent was already seeping from Real's remaining squad members. Asked if he would have sold Di Maria, Cristiano Ronaldo simply stated: 'If it was up to me, I wouldn't have done so.'

The Portuguese was one of Angel's closest friends in the Spanish capital, and Di Maria fittingly inherited the No.7 shirt which Ronaldo wore with such distinction during his six years in Manchester. 'I am aware of the importance of the number seven shirt,' Angel said at his press unveiling. 'Cristiano had spoken to me at Real Madrid and told me how important it was. There were a lot of clubs interested in me, but United is the only one that I would have left Real Madrid for. I am impressed by the vision and determination everyone has here to get this club back to the top – where it belongs.'

Having worked under managerial luminaries Mourinho and Ancelotti, the Argentinian confirmed that it was the chance to work under another which helped lead him to Manchester. 'Van Gaal was really important for me, in order to come here,' he said. 'He was one of the first who spoke about bringing me here. The coach always has the last word about the players he wants. I am really grateful to him because, thanks to him, I am now playing for United. I keep trying to improve every day and for that reason I wanted to come here to United. I needed to change my life. I will try my best to play the right way. I will try my best every match and show my arrival at Old Trafford was worth it.'

For United manager van Gaal, there is no doubt that the bumper fee will ultimately prove to be money well spent, having been impressed with Di Maria's character as well as his abilities on the field of play.

'I am very pleased that we can have such a class player in our squad,' he enthused. 'You have many class players but, for me, it is important that he is a team player. That is what I like in Di Maria, not only his class. He can accelerate the game for us but he can also play in the interest of the team. That is why we have chosen this player and I hope he shall give us good results. But we cannot expect after two days of training that he is the miracle, which is what I have already read [in the press]. You have to work for the miracle and he knows that.

'He fits into our philosophy. What he can do more to fit in our philosophy is that I can change the system with him and maybe we shall do that in the future. He played in Real Madrid not only as a wide wing player but also in midfield. That is also a reason why we are convinced that he shall succeed. I think he will be a player who the fans can enjoy and that is also a reason why we have chosen him.'

Procured for a club and national record fee, Di Maria's arrival represents the capture of an established star for United, bucking the trend of such talents leaving England for Spain. His early displays in Manchester provided a mouth-watering taste of his talents, and it seems inevitable that a feast of flavour lies ahead for the Reds' latest No.7.

8. JUAN MATA

Position: Midfielder
Born: 28 April 1988; Burgos, Spain
Previous clubs: Real Madrid (youth), Valencia, Chelsea
Joined United: 25 January 2014
Debut: 28 January 2014 vs Cardiff City (H), Premier League
Honours: None

A perennial thorn in United's side, Juan Mata appeared to be one of those 'I wish' players; an utterly likeable character with jaw-dropping ability, but apparently no means of ever being snaffled away from his current employers. The diminutive Spaniard – a class act on and off the field – was named Chelsea's Player of the Year in his first two seasons at Stamford Bridge and was beloved by Blues supporters. He appeared unmistakably unattainable.

Cue Jose Mourinho. The Portuguese's return to West London prompted a change in system for the Blues, with Mata's absence the sizeable price to pay for reshaping the team into his desired shape and style. Almost six months after being displaced, and mindful of the need to play his way into Spain's squad for the looming 2014 World Cup, Mata broached the possibility of leaving London, and United duly pounced to seal a then-club record £37.1 million deal.

'It was a hard decision,' admitted Mourinho, 'but to have a player in this situation is hard. He deserves that Chelsea open the door for him. He's very classy. I think he's a player that will stay in the fans' hearts and also in those of his colleagues.' His Old Trafford counterpart, meanwhile, was delighted to have wrapped up the signing of an established Premier League star from a perennial silverware rival. 'Juan is an undoubted talent who has had a good goalscoring record at every club he has played for,' beamed David Moyes. 'He is young enough to have a long career here at Manchester United and he is experienced enough to help us now and help improve the side. He is a player who I know our existing players are looking forward to working with as part of the squad.'

The Spaniard's arrival had a huge galvanising effect on the Aon Training Complex, with defender Phil Jones admitting: 'It makes an impact in the dressing room when you sign a player of that calibre. We want to impress and show him that we are what we are, that we are one of the best teams to be at.'

As entrances go, descent by helicopter makes a fairly striking statement. But if the grandiosity of Mata's arrival at United sat ill at ease with the Spaniard's humble nature, his enormous talent more than warranted it. The mammoth price tag bought United a thoroughbred talent, steeped in quality and with a rich history of success throughout his career for clubs and country. Born in Burgos, Spain and raised in Oviedo, he joined Real Madrid's youth academy at 15 and was in the same B-team as Alvaro Negredo, finishing second only to the former Manchester City striker in the 2006-07 scoring charts.

With his route to the first team blocked by the established creative forces of Robinho, Guti and Gonzalo Higuain, even before the arrival of Arjen Robben from Chelsea, Mata took the decision to join Valencia, where his first season brought instant success by culminating in Copa del Rey victory, in which he scored the opening goal against Michael Laudrup's Getafe in the final.

Silverware was new to the youngster at club level, but he could already draw on experience of it on the international stage, which would later become a recurring theme in his career. He had previously sampled success with Spain two years earlier at the European Under-19 Championships, where he scored five goals in four games. It would be on the international stage that he would enjoy tangible rewards for his efforts thereafter, as Valencia's form buckled under the burden of crippling debts which threatened the club's existence.

Although they continued to attain Champions League qualification over the following seasons, Davids Villa and Silva were sold to Barcelona and Manchester City respectively for bumper fees, just to keep Valencia afloat. But while Los Che's star quality dimmed with every major sale, Mata remained and became club captain for the duration of the 2010-11 campaign. By now a fringe member of Vicente Del Bosque's triumphant 2010 World Cup squad, he enjoyed further success as an overage player while Spain strode to the European Under-21 Championships. His reputation as one of

Europe's most gifted youngsters was cemented even before that triumph, and the continent's top clubs – including United – were all credited with an interest in Mata, before Chelsea ultimately secured his signature.

His maiden season in English football began with a debut goal against Norwich City and continued at a high standard before climaxing at club level with success in the FA Cup and the Champions League, as caretaker manager Roberto Di Matteo remarkably guided a side who had struggled domestically to the pinnacle of European football with a penalty shootout win over Bayern Munich in the Allianz Arena. Recognised by Chelsea's supporters with their Player of the Year award, Mata didn't dwell on the shock success; he simply moved on to more glory.

Just 11 days after Chelsea's triumph in Munich, Mata featured in Spain's pre-Euro 2012 friendly against South Korea, although his understandable exhaustion was quickly identified by the squad's medical team. But while his domestic exertions cost him the vast majority of the tournament, he still featured in the final. Introduced with three minutes remaining, by which point Spain were already 3-0 up against Italy, Mata needed only a minute to score, converting a Fernando Torres pass to round off the tournament's scoring.

He even managed to cram in a spot in Spain's short-lived involvement in the London Olympics ahead of the 2012-13 campaign, which once again yielded individual and collective silverware despite off-field tumult as Di Matteo departed the club with Rafael Benitez arriving in his stead on an interim basis. Chelsea ended the campaign clinching the Europa League, while Mata retained his Player of the Year award.

Yet, for all his success on the biggest stages at both club and international level, Juan found himself on the fringes of the action when Mourinho rejoined Chelsea after departing the Real Madrid hot seat. United moved swiftly upon learning of his availability, and his move to Manchester was quickly processed. 'Life is different from being in

London, which is a massive city, but I like it here,' he smiled. 'It is quiet, relaxed, a bit more countryside as well. But it's easier to get to the training ground. It's closer, just six minutes away if I go the back way!'

Already cup-tied in the Champions League and with United ousted from both domestic cup competitions, Mata was restricted to purely Premier League action in his opening few months at Old Trafford. Moyes departed the club just 92 days after signing the Spanish playmaker, but that was ample time for Mata to validate the Scot's substantial outlay with a string of impressive displays. A pair of sublime goals against Newcastle and another on the final day of the season at Southampton were the highlights of a six-goal showreel which also included a brace in Ryan Giggs's first game as interim manager. Though a seventh-place finish was not part of Mata's plan upon arriving, his ambitions remained undimmed for the future in both the short and long term.

'This season has been difficult for the club, for the players and obviously for me coming here, but I knew it wasn't going to be easy in the first months,' he said. 'I just tried to do, for example, what I did for two years at Chelsea. I was enjoying football, trying to score, trying to assist – that's the type of player I am, and I will always try to do the same. I will try to play my best. I know it was a big investment for the club, but I have confidence in myself. I believe in myself and know that I can do very well over these years. I was very happy with the welcome the club gave me, and the supporters, from the first day and on my debut, have been amazing. Since then, I am very happy and I am looking forward to winning trophies and being very successful with this club.'

His assimilation off the field has been hastened by two important factors. Firstly, his reputation as an intelligent footballer extends beyond the field of play. A bi-linguist who has juggled his playing career with degrees in sports science and marketing, Mata regularly updates his fans about his experiences on his own blog. Secondly, an influx of Spanish-speaking players has helped build a sizeable sub-group within the United squad. Falcao, Angel Di Maria, Marcos Rojo and Ander Herrera arrived in the summer of 2014, with the latter renewing acquaintances with Mata and David De Gea, both of whom had been his team-mates in Spain's youth ranks.

Not that any Hispanic cliques will be allowed to form at the Aon Training Complex, following the appointment of Louis van Gaal as manager. The summer arrival of the Dutchman, who insists all his players speak English to one another, provoked great excitement for Mata, whose positional wandering appeared at an end after regularly spending time on the left wing in his time under Moyes. In his early days at the club, van Gaal was quick to deploy the Spaniard in his favoured central position, pulling the Reds' creative strings behind two strikers.

'I hope it will be perfect for me,' said Mata. 'I feel comfortable in that position. I can play as a midfielder defensively or as a striker offensively if that's what I have to do. But my mission is always to assist and score. I can do that from this position and I hope I can have a great season. But more importantly it has to be a great season for the team. This system is difficult and it's difficult to adapt. You have to be very fit, for example. You have to be focused but, if you manage to master it, you can put lots of pressure on the opponent and you can hurt them with the ball. I think everyone knows that Dutch football likes to play a good way, a way I like to play and watch. This manager wants passing and movement and triangles. It's how I play my best.'

Van Gaal's relationship with his players is still in its infancy, having been delayed by the Netherlands' exploits at the 2014 World Cup in Brazil, but Mata was quickly impressed by the vastly experienced coach's impassioned methods. 'He is a manager who feels every session. Not just a game but a training session,' said the Spaniard. 'To him, it's all important. He is very into it. Sometimes he sees a striker or midfielder not make the right pass, he stops the session and tells them. He loves to do that. He is very temperamental.

'Everything he says is meant to help. You must have an open mind. If you are a professional player, that's basic. I have had many managers during the past years and I can learn from all of them. Now with Louis van Gaal we have a new way of working and we are all trying to adapt. Even the goalkeeper has an important role in the game-play.'

Having had time to settle after his move to Manchester, and standing as a big name of sufficient repute to match the glamour of the Reds' sparkling summer recruits, Mata looks likely to have a major part to play in van Gaal's Old Trafford revolution.

9. RADAMEL FALCAO

Position: Striker
Born: 10 February 1986; Santa Marta, Colombia
Previous clubs: River Plate, Porto, Atlético Madrid, Monaco
Joined United: 1 September 2014
Debut: 14 September 2014 vs Queens Park Rangers (H), Premier League
Honours: None

Radamel Falcao was just 13 years and 199 days old when he made his first appearance in senior football, wearing the colours of Colombian second division side Lanceros Boyacá in August 1999. By the age of 14, the teenage prodigy had registered six more senior outings and had come to terms with the idea that his future lay far away from his native land.

'He was a bit shy and the other players really didn't like what I did,' claims the team's coach, Hernán Pacheco, who took the unorthodox decision to field the youngster. 'Imagine having to come off for a thirteen-year-old kid? Both my guys and the opposition told me to stop messing around and treat football in a professional way, but they were all impressed after that game. We knew he was something special.'

Pacheco was correct in his assessment and, 15 years later, the boy from Santa Marta had grown into the 28-year-old powerhouse who stunned football with a transfer deadline-day move to United on a season-long loan from Monaco. While the road from Boyacá to Old Trafford was long and at times treacherous, Radamel's nomadic childhood has prepared him for the life of a professional footballer.

His father, Radamel García, was a sound centre-back who kept the family on their toes, playing for various clubs around Colombia and Venezuela. He was known for two things: his aggression in the tackle and his religious devotion – with just one trait passing down a generation. After calling his son Radamel, he also gave him the middle name Falcao after the great Brazil midfielder. Despite such admirable namesakes, it quickly became clear that Radamel Falcao García Zárate would not play in defence or midfield. He was a natural born centre-forward.

'I became a footballer almost by inheritance,' Falcao explains. 'My father was a professional player and he baptised me with a footballer's name and I accompanied him at all times during his career, so I always lived practically in that environment. He really wanted me to play, I think because he realised I was good enough. He enjoyed watching me play and saw that I had a future in this profession, so he helped me. What is important in my career is that I always had his support.'

At 15, having impressed for Lanceros Boyacá, Falcao moved to Argentina and joined River Plate for $500,000. While many Colombians had previously returned home at this stage, alone and scared of a strange city, Radamel showed a determination and tenacity that ultimately helped him settle in Buenos Aires. It is also here where the nickname 'El Tigre' was earned, after a team-mate told him he had played like a tiger during an Under-15s match. As monikers go, there are worse.

Unlike some aspiring players, his life was not all about football and he decided to study journalism at university – something he has in common with United's fellow literary students Ander Herrera and Juan Mata. Thankfully, Falcao could kick a ball with considerable prowess and a debut for River arrived in the final game of the 2004-05 season. By the start of the new campaign, he was a regular in the team and scored seven goals in as many games. His momentum stalled, however, when he twice injured the ligaments in his right knee, with the second blow prompting the first surgery of his career. At this time, his faith helped him through the rehabilitation process and, coincidentally, it was at church that he met his wife Lorelei Taron – an Argentinian singer.

Following a slow but steady recovery, Falcao reclaimed his scoring touch under the management of Diego Simeone and held a record of 34 goals in 90 games by the end of the 2008-09 season. But due to River's financial problems, a £3.5 million transfer to Porto was sanctioned and Radamel was en route to Europe – just a year after a speculative bid from Aston Villa was rejected.

The Colombian hit the ground running in Portugal and scored in each of his first four games, before lifting the Portuguese Cup at the end of his first season. The following campaign provided another step up as Andre Villas Boas led Porto to the league title without suffering a single defeat. The Cup was also retained, before Falcao's solitary goal against Primeira Liga rivals Braga claimed the Europa League and a historic treble. By this point, his eye-catching form had caught the attention of bigger fish.

'After a very successful season in Porto, I thought it was the right time to make the leap to a major league,' said Falcao, when discussing his €40 million transfer to La Liga side Atlético Madrid, who had bought him as a replacement for Manchester City-bound Sergio Aguero. 'I wanted the challenge to go to Spain and play in one of the best leagues in the world with the best players. Atlético gave me the chance to try to fight with the bigger teams, to try to reach the

Champions League and to win the Europa League again. There were some offers from different parts of Europe, but in the end I chose Atlético because they were the ones that showed that they wanted me and made a big effort to bring me in.'

True to their word, the Spanish outfit – taken over by former River boss Simeone midway through Falcao's debut season – helped the striker become the first player in history to win consecutive Europa League titles with different sides. Perhaps more impressively, the feat was achieved via an impressively comfortable 3-0 win over Ander Herrera's Athletic Club, with the Colombian scoring twice in the showpiece finale to deservedly claim the Man-of-the-Match champagne.

As Chelsea supporters might remember all too well, his 2012-13 campaign began with a stylish first-half hat-trick during a 4-1 win over Roberto Di Matteo's European champions in the UEFA Super Cup final. As the *Guardian* wrote that night, 'Blues owner Roman Abramovich had come to Monte Carlo hoping to watch his team hoist silverware again and set the tone for the months ahead. He must have departed with Falcao playing on his mind.'

Falcao's trophy cabinet was later bolstered by a 2013 Copa del Rey winner's medal at the end of another fruitful season in front of goal, with his Atlético record standing tall at 52 in 67 outings. With such impressive numbers, the striker was arguably the hottest property in world football at that time and mega-rich Monaco's attention was predictably captured. The club's Russian billionaire owner, Dmitry Rybolovlev, was determined to land a marquee signing following the team's promotion to Ligue 1 and tabled a €60 million offer that was quickly accepted, allowing a lucrative five-year contract to be signed by the end of May. For all the surprise at Falcao eschewing Champions League football to move to Monaco, he maintained his white-hot form by hitting 11 in his first 17 matches. But then disaster struck.

On 22 January 2014, Falcao suffered more anterior cruciate ligament damage in his right knee during a 3-0 French Cup win at

Chasselay Monts d'or Azergues and was ruled out for the remainder of the season. Despite undergoing surgery that enabled a tentative return in June, his recovery was not swift enough to earn a place in Colombia's 23-man squad for the World Cup in Brazil – a seismic blow for both player and country, considering he had scored nine goals in qualifying. 'I was very excited but now I'll have to support the team from afar and I wish them well, hoping they play a good World Cup,' he told Colombian newspaper *El Pais*. Poignantly, having made the decisive call, a devastated José Pékerman declared it 'the saddest day I've had since becoming Colombia coach'.

Falcao's much-anticipated return finally happened in July, ironically on English soil at the Emirates Stadium, where his comeback goal earned a 1-0 pre-season success over Arsenal. Little did he know it, but the fit-again striker would soon return to these shores in entirely different circumstances. Indeed, with just minutes remaining of the summer transfer window, which had already been extended by two hours at United's request, the club reached agreement with Monaco for a sensational season-long loan move that would see the 28-year-old join the Louis van Gaal revolution at Old Trafford.

After concluding what was undoubtedly the highlight of a frantic deadline day, van Gaal explained how the opportunity to bolster his forward line with such quality was just too good to turn down. 'I am delighted Radamel has joined us on loan this season,' he said. 'He is one of the most prolific goalscorers in the game. His appearance-to-goal ratio speaks for itself and, when a player of this calibre becomes available, it is an opportunity not to be missed.'

Despite arriving at the Aon Training Complex in the late afternoon, Falcao did not have confirmation of his temporary switch until exactly 01:30 BST. While confident that everything was in hand, the devout Christian admittedly tapped into his faith for reassurances as the clock ticked into the small hours. 'I am very happy to be part of this big club,' he told MUTV. 'I've waited for this moment during a lot of the year. Now I am a player of Manchester United. It was a very long day. It was hard, difficult. We were waiting until the last minute but I didn't lose my faith. Now I want to say thank you to God for this. I'm very happy. I am very excited to work with van Gaal, who is a very good trainer with a lot of experience. I want to do the best for the team, for him and for the supporters.'

Fans were understandably enthused by the announcement and marvelled at the prospect of Falcao linking up with £59.7 million club-record signing Angel Di Maria, who had signed on the dotted line just six days earlier. Both moves were welcomed by strikers Wayne Rooney and Robin van Persie, who spoke of improvements on the pitch following a slow start to the season. Perhaps more impressively, club legend Paul Scholes was similarly supportive of the acquisition and looked forward to seeing some South American swagger at the Theatre of Dreams.

'The calibre of player we have brought in is top quality, with Di Maria and Falcao,' Scholes explained in September. 'These are proper players. We just have to find a way of getting them all in the same team, playing well and scoring goals – which we have struggled to do a little bit. Falcao's goalscoring record is brilliant from when he has been at Porto and Atlético Madrid. The goals he has scored have been important. Then there is also the movement he brings and his experience as well at twenty-eight years of age. You just hope his knee is right, but once he gets going and Di Maria can start creating chances for him then I'm sure we will start scoring goals.'

While facing the media during his official unveiling as a United player, the new No.9 offered assurances that his knee problems were behind him, explaining that he felt fit and ready to fire the Reds back to glory. 'I feel well. I started to play two months ago with Monaco and I've improved in the last month a lot,' he said. 'I have scored goals and that's important to a striker. I am confident with my phys-ical form and I am comfortable with my knee. I feel very good in myself and I am very happy to be here. I've had a great welcome. When you talk about a settling-in period, it makes it very easy when you are surrounded by quality players. I can't wait to get started.'

Having travelled from Colombia's second division to the world's biggest football club, United's loan star has seemingly found his home at Old Trafford. 'I hope to stay here for many years and make history at this club,' he reassured supporters. 'When I was in Porto and Madrid, I always wanted to improve and I dreamt about playing in a team like this. Now, I want to stay here for many years.'

10. WAYNE ROONEY

Position: Striker
Born: 24 October 1985; Liverpool, England
Previous club: Everton
Joined United: 31 August 2004
Debut: 28 September 2004 vs Fenerbahce (H), Champions League
Honours: Premier League (2006-07, 2007-08, 2008-09, 2010-11, 2012-13), UEFA Champions League (2007-08), FIFA Club World Cup (2008), League Cup (2005-06, 2009-10), Community Shield (2007, 2010, 2011)

For all the years spent indoctrinating young footballers with the Manchester United way, every so often, another club produces a player who looks born to represent the Reds. Wayne Rooney was one such instance.

The pugnacious, all-action youngster was still 17 days shy of his 17th birthday when he made his first appearance at Old Trafford, thrown on by Everton manager David Moyes as a late substitute. The hard-fought Monday evening game was goalless when Rooney entered the fray with 16 minutes remaining, and he needed less than five minutes to make an impact, picking up on a loose ball, charging past three United defenders and forcing Fabien Barthez into a smart save. Though the hosts ultimately took the spoils with three late goals, the youngster had made an impression and, 12 days later, he struck his first Premier League goal – a 25-yarder, in injury time, via the crossbar, to account for champions Arsenal, no less.

Rooney's penchant for the spectacular was already well known to Sir Alex Ferguson and his staff, however; he had first surfaced on the Reds' radar eight years earlier. Paul McGuinness, now United's Under-18s coach, had taken charge of the newly formed Under-9s for their first-ever game, against an Everton side containing a future household name.

'We hadn't played any games before, the boys had just been training together,' said McGuinness. 'We didn't even have a goal-keeper, so Peter Schmeichel's son Kasper played for us. He was the only kid we knew who played in goal! The Everton boys had been playing together for at least a year in a league beforehand, so they were used to playing games. You could tell, because they absolutely hammered us.

'He scored a few (six to be exact), but there was one goal that stood out. It was basically the classic overhead kick, the perfect bicycle kick, which for a kid of eight or nine years old was really something special. We were all wondering who this kid was. It transpired that he was from a tough, boxing background, a sporting family and he was a diehard Everton fan. At that time you didn't really get any kids crossing over to Manchester from Liverpool. We looked at it behind the scenes, but he was too fixated on Everton to contemplate leaving them.'

Rooney had scored half of Everton's goals in a 12-2 obliteration of the Reds at Littleton Road, and McGuinness duly informed Ferguson that he had come across a boy with a special talent. There would be regular opportunities to check on the prodigy's progress over the ensuing years, as he continued to cross paths with United's sides as he rose up through Everton's ranks. The scouting reports weren't always positive – Rooney was sent off for scuffling with Reds defender Mark Howard in an Under-13s game – but there was always a sense of dormant brilliance, even when the bull-necked youngster wasn't at his best.

Tommy Martin, manager of United's Under-15s, can vividly remember Everton's No.9 terrorising the Reds' backline in one meeting. 'Overall we were too strong for them, but he stood out on their side,' he recalled. 'Wayne gave our defence a really tough time. After ten or fifteen minutes, you knew he was on the pitch because he was really upsetting our defenders. His pace always made him a handful. He was a winner back then – you could tell. Even back then he was going back and tackling. He's always been in love with the game of football.'

'I remember sitting with [Academy consultant] Jim Ryan watching him at Altrincham,' added McGuinness. 'We won the game five-one, but I remember Jim saying: "Look at their number nine, he's keeping at it and going all the time." He was running around after the ball and trying shots, and he really stood out in that game. We started following him closely from that point.'

According to United's chief recruitment officer Geoff Watson, however, the Reds' keen interest was fuelled by Everton's complete assurance that Rooney was destined for the top. 'The important thing that struck me was that when you spoke to the Everton people they were always so confident that they had a star in the making,' he said. 'They were so convinced about Wayne's ability. It was obvious he was a special talent. So many people went to watch Wayne Rooney that it was easy to get an opinion about him, there was a big buzz about him. Everton knew what they'd got from an early age.'

Rooney was still at an early age when he announced himself to the Premier League, and less than two years later, United moved for him on the back of a stunning Euro 2004 campaign with England. The striker, who initially took the No.8 shirt at Old Trafford, became football's most expensive teenager with the transfer – a record he kept until the summer of 2014, when United ensnared Luke Shaw from Southampton.

A broken foot sustained on international duty was no deterrent to the Reds, who were happy to wait for the 18-year-old's debut. And it was worth it. Rooney needed just 17 minutes to open his account, and 54 minutes to become only the second player in the club's history to score a hat-trick on his debut. His treble against Fenerbahce remains a Champions League record for the youngest hat-trick scorer in the competition's history, and at the time created an inevitable storm of hype.

'The Messiah has come to Manchester and this time there are no doubters, no nay-sayers, no prophets of doom,' wrote the *Daily Mail's* Jeff Powell. 'Wayne Rooney looks like a gift from the gods. The latest Cantona? Make that the new Best. Only this time he is English and Wayne's World Cup is beckoning, too. George the Greatest crowned a team of football princes. Rooney's arrival transformed half a team of reserves into a regal force. Fenerbahce made a game of it, but this was not so much a football match as the anointing of a saviour.'

Once the dust had settled, Rooney's integration continued at a more natural pace. United ended his maiden campaign – 2004-05 – without a trophy, but his all-round displays and penchant for spectacular goals augured well for the future. There were occasional issues over temperament, and his first red card followed in 2005-06 when he responded to a booking by sarcastically applauding Danish referee Kim Milton Nielsen, but the early years of Rooney's United career served up largely joyous fare.

His brace helped United to a resounding win over Wigan in the 2005-06 League Cup final and secured the youngster his first piece of silverware, and the drip would soon become a torrent. Rooney and Cristiano Ronaldo had developed in tandem under Ferguson, but an international spat between the pair at the 2006 World Cup was tipped to tear United apart. Rather, the duo starred as Jose Mourinho's all-conquering Chelsea were prevented from winning a third straight title, and the United pair picked up their very first.

Rooney's next step was to swap shirts, upgrading to his preferred No.10 which had gone unworn for a season after Ruud van Nistelrooy's departure. 'Ten has always been my favourite number,' he said. 'When Ruud left and no one took it the following season, I asked the manager and David Gill if I could have the shirt. I had to wait a year, but it's great. Great players who scored so many goals for the club have worn this shirt, so I knew what a big number it was for me to take. But that history makes wearing the shirt feel even better and also makes it more of a challenge to succeed.'

Fate decreed that United's new No.10 duly suffered a broken foot in the opening game of the 2007-08 campaign. Once again, however, what followed would be worth the wait, and Rooney provided an integral presence as the Reds retained the Premier League title and overcame Chelsea in the first ever all-English Champions League final. His fruitful partnership with Carlos Tevez was disrupted during the following term, after the club record purchase of Dimitar Berbatov and with Ronaldo increasingly used in a central role, but still Rooney kept scoring. He topped the 20-goal mark for only the second time in 2008-09, but it was the subsequent departure of Ronaldo to Real Madrid which liberated the England international to become the focal point of United's attack.

'I don't think the responsibility of getting more goals will affect Wayne,' predicted Ferguson. 'He has the mental strength for all that. He will be used through the middle this season. And he is maturing and he will improve. When we signed him as a kid, we thought he would become a really top player. Without question he is going in that direction. He is blessed with some ingredients only great foot-ballers have. He has a great determination and hunger to win every match and every training session. That will never change. He plays as if he means it. It is a wonderful thing to have. If he can score more consistently over the season he will get to twenty-five and above.'

Not for the first time, Ferguson's shrewd judgement was spot on. Rooney enjoyed his best goalscoring return to date, notching a staggering 34 goals before suffering an ankle injury against Bayern Munich which decimated both his and United's season. A winner in the League Cup final victory over Aston Villa and the PFA Player of the Year award was all the striker had to show for a sterling year's work, and his frustration continued through to the following season, when he stunned the club by submitting a transfer request which he promptly withdrew after discussions with Ferguson and chief executive David Gill.

'Sometimes as a player you make bad choices and bad decisions, and I think that's what happened,' Rooney later reflected. 'I spoke with the manager and David Gill and then I went home and I was sat there thinking "Right, what's the plan?" I knew I'd made a mistake and I went back in and told them I'd made a mistake.'

From the brink of an exit, Rooney suddenly penned a new, five-year contract and ended the season on a high, hitting the penalty against Blackburn Rovers which confirmed United's record 19th league title, before scoring in a Champions League final defeat to Pep Guardiola's unstoppable Barcelona. The following year was far more settled for the striker, and he matched his personal best haul of 34 goals, only for Manchester City to pilfer the title on goal difference in the final seconds of the campaign.

Rooney's rollercoaster ride continued as his frustration spilled over into the 2012-13 term, when he suffered a horrific gashed leg against Fulham in his first game of the campaign and was forced back onto the sidelines. His subsequent search for form, allied to the incredible impact of new signing Robin van Persie, meant that his future was again the subject of speculation even amid United's 20th title celebrations. The subsequent replacement of Ferguson with

David Moyes, however, provided a new lease of life for the striker.

'When David Moyes took over he made it clear to me straight away that he wanted to draw a line under last season,' said Rooney. 'And the key thing was when he assured me that he had total belief in me. Just as important, he also told me things that I probably didn't want to hear. He told me I had lost something from my game and that I needed to get back to basics. The boss reminded me about the player I was. He wanted to know what had happened to all my aggression. He said that I'd lost something important from my game – and he wanted it back.'

It returned in a sensational opening spell of the 2013-14 term for Rooney, who demonstrated his enduring excellence and was rewarded with another long-term deal – and the promise of a club ambassadorial role after his retirement – midway through the campaign. Though Moyes would not last the entire campaign, the return of Rooney's mojo was emphatic enough to convince the Scot's replacement, Louis van Gaal, that the Merseysider was the right man to replace the departed Nemanja Vidic as club captain.

'For me it's always very important the choice of captain,' said the Dutchman. 'Wayne has shown a great attitude towards everything he does. I have been very impressed by his professionalism and his attitude to training and to my philosophy. He is a great inspiration to the younger members of the team and I believe he will put his heart and soul into his captaincy role.'

'It gives me great pride and it's a great honour for me to captain the team,' added Rooney. 'I spoke to the manager and he decided that I was right to take the role, which I am delighted with. I will perform the role as best I can and hopefully help the team to be successful. Then I'll try to lead the players on the pitch with hard work, dedication, and that's what we really want to do – we want to show the fans that we care and want to win.'

Armband or not, Rooney has been leading by example for years at Old Trafford. Now, his aim is to lead van Gaal's new-look Reds back to the splendour which underscored the vast majority of his glorious first decade at the club.

11. ADNAN JANUZAJ

Position: Attacker
Born: 5 February 1995; Brussels, Belgium
Previous club: Anderlecht (youth)
Joined: 1 July 2011
Debut: 11 August 2013 vs Wigan Athletic (N), Community Shield
Honours: Community Shield (2013)

The raised stakes within modern football mean that the battles to enlist the best young talents are often fierce affairs. For Adnan Januzaj, however, United were not required to sell themselves as a destination, for the gifted trickster was set on ignoring all other alternatives in favour of moving to Manchester.

When the Reds' Belgian-based scout Alex Verveckken first contacted the club in August 2010, after witnessing Januzaj in action for Anderlecht in a youth tournament at KV Mechelen in Belgium, the club sent several members of the Academy's staff to cast their eye over the youngster. 'It meant everybody pulling together,' said Geoff Watson, United's regional and European recruitment officer.

'All of us were impressed with what we saw, and we recommended that the Academy should try to sign him as soon as possible. The general opinion was that Adnan was a player with very high potential. With signing such players, things are rarely easy, but this one was different. Adnan only wanted to sign for Manchester United and that's the truth. There was loads of competition – there is all the time – and the boy and his family deserve full credit for the fact that they just wanted to come to Manchester United. It was a real coup for the Academy.'

Less pleased was Jean Kinderman, Anderlecht's head of youth development. 'Adnan made a big impression – such a talent you don't see every year,' he said. 'He stood out because of his technical skills, his protection of the ball, the fact that he is always standing up, that he has a fantastic sense of the game. He was physically very, very small when we lost him three seasons ago. Now I see a real athlete – when he left here he was a young boy. He chose the most difficult project. If he stayed here in Anderlecht, he would play today in our first team and it could be a trampoline to Europe. We are proud, of course, but a little disappointed because he left too early.'

The battle to secure Januzaj's services on the international stage was by no means as straightforward as his choice of club, with five countries vying for his attention. Born in Brussels, Adnan is the son of Kosovar-Albanian parents who fled the Balkan crisis, while his Turkish grandparents offered another international alternative, as did the chance to represent England through five years' residency in Manchester. Ultimately, the highly rated youngster plumped for Belgium, the country of his birth, to bring closure to a saga which played out in public ever since his Reds debut in 2013-14.

Adnan became an overnight sensation following his first senior start, in October 2013, in which he hit a brilliant, match-winning brace in United's 2-1 win at Sunderland, but the teenager had required boundless patience prior to his dramatic emergence. After moving to Manchester in March 2011, Januzaj was immediately delayed by bureaucratic issues. 'I had to wait for the paperwork to come through on the transfer,' he said. 'It was just a case of training hard, even though I wasn't playing, and just thinking: "I don't know but maybe tomorrow it will come through." So I was just hoping to do my best.'

Sidelined for the remainder of the 2010-11 campaign and the start of the following season, Adnan finally made his bow for Paul McGuinness's Under-18s in October 2011 – seven months after signing – and he adapted commendably quickly, catching the eye in roles as a striker and a support striker. Just 11 outings into his Reds career, however, he sustained a serious knee injury which required lengthy rehabilitation, including a spell at Nike HQ in Portland.

'I had never had an injury before and that was the first one,' recalled Januzaj. 'You learn a lot when you are injured. The gym helps as well because you are getting stronger and doing different things that are all parts of football. So it was actually a good experience, even if I hope not to be injured again! After that, I came back and wanted to show the coaches what I could do.'

Eric Harrison, coach of the famed Class of '92 and a regular attendee at United's youth fixtures, was among those immediately smitten with the youngster. 'The first time I saw him was in a youth game and he was outstanding. Then you get excited and realise he's one for the future,' said Harrison. 'Everybody at the club knows that he is definitely one for the future. He's going to be a big asset to the club.'

That asset was only briefly available to the club's youth coaches. Just six days after making his debut for Warren Joyce's Reserves against Accrington Stanley in August 2012's Lancashire Senior Cup final, Januzaj travelled with Sir Alex Ferguson's senior squad to a pre-season friendly at Aberdeen, where his 45-minute cameo stood out. Quinton Fortune, one of his team-mates at Pittodrie, admitted: 'Everyone knew that he was special. Adnan was making so much progress and when he went to train with the first team, the lads were talking about him.'

Across the 2012-13 campaign proper, Januzaj impressed regularly for Joyce's Under-21s while occasionally turning out for the Under-18s, and he operated mainly as a striker. Yet, despite playing outside his comfort zone, being naturally suited to wide positions and harbouring a preference to start as a No.10, Adnan's potential was underlined when Ferguson labelled him a 'definite Manchester United first-team player'.

In the same week that he picked up the Denzil Haroun Reserve Team Player of the Year award for 2012-13, Januzaj's displays earned further reward with a shock call-up to Ferguson's final squad as United manager: the 5-5 draw with West Bromwich Albion, which he watched as an unused substitute.

It was Ferguson's replacement, David Moyes, who gave Adnan his break, naming the Belgian in his first team selection against Thailand's Singha All-Stars. Januzaj went on to appear in each leg of the Reds' pre-season tour of Asia and Australia, before making his competitive bow in the Community Shield victory over Wigan Athletic.

A substitute in home meetings with Crystal Palace, Liverpool and West Brom, Januzaj was creating a buzz that grew incrementally each time he picked up possession. Blessed with bravery, purpose and skill, his talent naturally struck a chord with an Old Trafford audience entertained by some of the very best. It was on enemy turf, though, that Januzaj came to the fore with a match-winning full debut at Sunderland, a display embossed by two classy finishes which, while stunning in their execution, were no surprise to his manager.

'Starting Adnan certainly wasn't a gamble for me,' insisted Moyes. 'I see him in training every day, I saw him on tour and actually he's even got better since coming back. He's looked as good as anybody in training, so I thought he deserved to play. I remember giving Wayne Rooney and Ross Barkley their debuts and Adnan is certainly in that quality.'

One of the millstones young players often have to bear is comparisons with their forebears, but the confidence of Januzaj prohibits him from wilting under any associated pressure. Likened in some respects to Cristiano Ronaldo, Adnan simply admitted: 'I watch him a lot and try to do the same things that he does. He is a very good player. I always look at him and watch his games as well and try to do what he is doing and remember what he did at Manchester United. I have to work hard in the gym like he did because, when he came here, he wasn't strong. But after a year or so he became really strong and could push people away. I'm getting a bit stronger now due to the gym work.'

Elsewhere in the United ranks, even leading lights such as Robin van Persie can see aspects of themselves in the quicksilver starlet. 'When I go back ten years to when I was quite young, I see similar attributes,' said the Dutchman. 'He's confident in a good way. He's not too bothered with the whole occasion or the pressure of the games. I was very confident as well and I see some stuff in him and the choices he makes that I made when I was younger as well. But he's not the new van Persie, he's the new Adnan. He's a great player and I'm a great fan of his. I thought earlier in pre-season that he has something special. He will give Manchester United a great bunch of goals and great games. He's a special player.'

Januzaj, who made just 39 appearances throughout his rise through the club's youth system, amassed 35 senior outings in 2013-14, and though the campaign was collectively difficult for United, who replaced Moyes with Louis van Gaal as manager, Adnan confided: 'I am quite pleased with my year, I have done a lot of work and have been integrating into the first team. I have played games and I think there is more to come. I hope to win trophies at this club and be the best player.'

The 2014-15 term began for Januzaj with a piece of history, as he inherited the Reds' famous No.11 shirt after the retirement of Ryan Giggs, and the Belgian was typically unflustered by the associated expectations of becoming only the second wearer of the shirt since the advent of Premier League squad numbers. 'It was a big honour for me and my family and I was very happy to have it given to me,' he said. 'There is pressure on me because there was a legend in front of me who had it for twenty years, but I am really happy with that. I feel privileged. I used to watch him. I learnt a lot of things from him; there are so many things that, really, I could not make a list!'

Adnan's wasn't the only notable squad number to change hands, with Angel Di Maria and Radamel Falcao taking No.7 and No.9 respectively. Some onlookers cited the arrival of such stellar talents as

143

blockades along the road of Januzaj's development, but both the player and his manager insist to the contrary. Van Gaal trialled the Belgian in a central midfield role in pre-season, introduced him as a left-winger on the season-opening defeat to Swansea and in various positions as a second-half substitute in the Capital One Cup setback against MK Dons. Where there is a talent as rich as Januzaj's, it will force its own accommodation.

Nevertheless, Adnan felt it important that he speak out to quickly curtail any whispers of discontent, stressing: 'Number ten is my preferred position, but I'm happy to play anywhere for the manager. I saw some reports saying I was unhappy. That couldn't be further from the truth. I love this club and I'm excited to play for this manager. The fans have been so good to me and I want to repay them.'

At a club where the currency comes in denominations of excitement, unpredictability and entertainment, Januzaj has a wealth of talent at his disposal. Repaying the supporters who sing his name with such affection is not likely to prove difficult for such a prodigiously gifted young player with a genuine affection for his club.

12. CHRIS SMALLING

Position: Defender
Born: 22 November 1989; Greenwich, England
Previous clubs: Maidstone United, Fulham
Joined United: 7 July 2010
Debut: 8 August 2010 vs Chelsea (N), Community Shield
Honours: Premier League (2010-11, 2012-13), Community Shield (2010, 2011, 2013)

On 28 January 2010, Chris Smalling signed for Manchester United to complete a meteoric rise from the depths of non-league football to the glamour of the Premier League champions in just two short years. What made his arrival at Old Trafford even more remarkable was the presence of Arsenal in the hunt for his much sought-after signature, which forced the boyhood Gunners fan to turn his back on Arsene Wenger following a couple of influential meetings with Reds manager Sir Alex Ferguson, whose reputation for developing young English talent eventually proved decisive.

Chris first learned of United's interest from his then boss at Fulham, Roy Hodgson, who pulled him aside the night before the Cottagers' match at Blackburn Rovers, 12 days before the transfer was completed. The current England manager said an offer for him had been accepted and that Ferguson would be arriving in 40 minutes to meet him. 'I only just had time to ring my mum to say I was going to be meeting him and then he was there,' Smalling recalled. 'It was just a bit surreal, but he even rang my mum and my mum recognised straight away who it was. That was nice.'

'I was just so shocked. It was the voice,' explained Chris's mother, Theresa, when quizzed on her unexpected phone call. 'It was like I was on TV. He was just saying how impressed he was with Chris, how he'll be well looked after and telling me about everything they've got up there. I couldn't believe it when Chris said about Manchester United. I'm an Arsenal fan and Chris was when he was little, but I'm so proud of him.'

Wenger did his best, too, and forced Smalling to make an incredibly difficult decision for somebody who has endured so few winters. 'I did have a phone conversation,' Smalling later admitted. 'He said what he thought, in terms of what I could go on to do, and it was more left to me in terms of going away and thinking about it. It was a difficult decision. Those few days were some of the hardest I've had in my career. You do have to think about it. You have to weigh it up.'

But the meeting with Sir Alex, which was followed by another nine days later, was successful. Smalling recalls the Scottish accent and his own sweaty palms, but surprisingly it was the lure of playing with somebody who would block his path into the first team for both club and country that informed his choice. 'I already had a gut feeling that I wanted to go to United,' he said. 'Once I'd got to meet Sir Alex and was able to speak to him about his vision for me, I knew. With a club like this there was only one thought. And in terms of some of the other players here: there's an English core and that was great. The idea of linking up with Rio Ferdinand really appealed.'

Smalling's ability to make difficult decisions with absolute calm is undoubtedly linked to the relaxed manner in which he leads his life. Always one step ahead of the game, it takes a lot to knock the talented defender off balance. What is also noticeable about Chris is the way he speaks with a maturity beyond his years, an attribute that is perhaps linked to the fact he was only five when his father, Lloyd, sadly passed away.

'I don't remember much about him,' Smalling explained, while discussing his late father. 'I was five, my brother was three and it was an unfortunate thing, but my mum has brought us up and we've stayed close ever since. Mum put a lot of focus on me and my brother and I think at times we both probably got a bit annoyed with her saying, "You've got to do this before you go and play on the PlayStation", or whatever. It's paid off, though.'

Shortly after his dad's passing, the Smalling family moved from Greenwich to a modest semi-detached house in Chatham, Kent, where Chris and his younger brother Jason were enrolled at the local Walderslade Boys Club. It was here where he developed a love for judo, a sport that he flourished in until football later took precedence at the age of 16.

'One of my big passions has always been judo,' said Smalling. 'I've competed since I was five, competed from the age of six or seven until I was a sixteen-year-old and was also national champion for my age group. When my family moved from Greenwich to Chatham, it was walking distance to the local Walderslade judo club, so I went down a few times a week. I remember when I became national champion competing in an international – in Norwich if I recall – only losing to a Polish guy who was a bit stronger than me. It was pretty tight – he had me in a hold I couldn't get out of. I got a few medals, though when I got to England schoolboy level at football I had to put that on hold. But I still like watching the sport and I sometimes speak to Eddie, my coach at Walderslade.'

After showing promise in the local Medway leagues, Smalling joined Millwall when he was 12, but travelling to London proved too much by the time he had reached 14. Ms Smalling, a single mum, didn't have a car and, although Millwall offered to fund his commute, she didn't want her teenage son travelling on his own. 'We just couldn't get up there,' she said. 'He would have been perfectly capable of going on his own, but I wouldn't let him. I had to take him out. He didn't play football for nearly a year. I was more upset than Chris, I think. He just carried on and worked his way up, playing for school and then Kent. He really put himself out there.' Thankfully, his time would come.

While studying for his A Levels at Chatham Grammar School for Boys (later earning three Bs and a C) and holding down a job as a waiter at a local hotel, Smalling was forcing his way into the Maidstone United first team. After impressing the relevant people at the Gallagher Stadium, he started the 2007-08 season playing against the mighty Whitstable and regularly drove to training in his beloved Renault Clio, which had already seen better days. More importantly, his talent was shining through. 'When you've been in football for a long time, sometimes you see a little gem,' explained Bill Williams, Maidstone's general manager who had previously played for QPR, Portsmouth and West Brom. 'The first one I ever had was Bruce Grobbelaar when he was seventeen or eighteen. You know that they are special players. And Chris was one of them.'

As reserve team manager Tony Cornwell observed, Smalling's

natural ability was destined to transport him to the top. 'He always had time, he was an elegant player, he played out from the centre of defence, he liked to pass the ball, he could read the game superbly well,' said Cornwell. 'His physical attributes are great and he's quick. But we were playing games in the Ryman Premier and he was Man of the Match every week. He was absolutely outstanding. He could play anywhere across the back four and even played in midfield at Under-18 level. But central defence is his best position. He reminds me of Rio Ferdinand with the way he plays.'

At 17, Smalling was called up for England Schoolboys, which caught the attention of scouts from Middlesbrough, Charlton, Reading, Fulham, Chelsea and Arsenal. Mother and son liked what they saw when they visited the Riverside Stadium and Smalling nearly signed on the dotted line, but the promise of a three-year deal much closer to home at Fulham proved more attractive. The Cottagers' senior scout, Barry Dunn, now head of youth recruitment at Millwall, had got his man. And due to the fact that Smalling had never signed a contract with Maidstone, the Premier League outfit had no legal obligation to pay a penny when the move was finalised in the summer of 2008.

'Because of the relationship between the two clubs, with Hodgson being a former Maidstone player, Fulham gave us what they call a training compensation agreement, which is registered with the FA,' explained Williams. 'At the time it was a great deal and we appreciated it. However, in the general scheme of things, it isn't so good. In your wildest dreams, nobody thought somebody would pay that amount of money at this stage in Chris's career. It would have been nice if we had had a ten per cent sell-on, which we asked for, because we've been striving for fifteen years to build a stadium in the town and that money would've done it. I think they call it Sod's Law, don't they?'

Smalling went on to make just 13 senior appearances for the Craven Cottage club before moving to Old Trafford in the summer of 2010 ready to begin his new adventure under Ferguson, who was confident he had found a diamond in the rough. 'Roy Hodgson developed a high regard for him at Fulham,' the former Reds manager wrote in his bestselling autobiography. 'He cost us around £10 million. We moved for him when Rio Ferdinand started having problems with his back and other parts. We were on to centre-backs everywhere, all over. We watched them all through 2009-10 and thought Smalling was a young guy who would mature into his frame. Long term, I could imagine a central defence forming around Chris Smalling and Jonny Evans.'

The versatile defender made 33 appearances during his first season at United, winning the title and playing in a Champions League semi-final victory over Schalke. His second term, which was preceded by the arrival of Phil Jones from Blackburn, saw him experience heartache as Manchester City claimed the championship on goal difference, though things were eventually put right when the Premier League trophy was brought back to Old Trafford at the end of Ferguson's final campaign as manager.

By this point in his career, Smalling was learning his craft after reaping the benefits of working with Ferdinand and his iconic defensive partner, Nemanja Vidic. 'It's been massive for me,' he conceded. 'Before I even came here they were two of the best centre-backs around. It's a privilege to be able to train and work with them – you learn so much, even just in conversations in the dressing room when they've given me great little bits of advice and knowledge which has helped with my development.'

While many people were keen to forget the 2013-14 season, Smalling aims to maintain the consistency that allowed him to register his highest total of appearances (38) for a single campaign and feels confident that his career is heading in the right direction. Having made a steady start under new manager Louis van Gaal, with just a slight injury disrupting his rhythm at the start of this term, the England international looks set for a bright future at the Theatre of Dreams.

Smalling has also come a long way since lining up for lowly Maidstone. He now lives in a luxury house that he has bought in Cheshire, just 15 minutes away from the Aon Training Complex, which is significant step up from his childhood. While his beloved Renault Clio is also a thing of the past, with a sleeker number parked on the driveway, he remains as polite and humble as the day he first arrived at Old Trafford in the summer of 2010.

The former non-league dreamer is also acutely aware of how precious his opportunities are at United. 'I'd like to think I wouldn't get too carried away and will always appreciate what I've got,' he explained, with one eye on the future. 'I know that not long ago I didn't have much, after all.'

13. ANDERS LINDEGAARD

Position: Goalkeeper
Born: 13 April 1984; Dyrup, Denmark
Previous clubs: Odense Boldklub, Kolding FC (loan), Aalesunds FK
Joined United: 4 January 2011
Debut: 29 January 2011 vs Southampton (A), FA Cup
Honours: Premier League (2012-13), Community Shield (2011, 2013)

When legendary goalkeeper Peter Schmeichel lifted the Champions League trophy in 1999, drawing the curtain on his astonishing Manchester United career in the most dramatic, glorious circumstances, Anders Lindegaard was just 15 years old and cheering on his hero back in Denmark.

A United fan from the age of four, after encouragement from his Reds-supporting father, Anders' idolisation of Schmeichel was inevitable, as was a preference for keeping goal. Seeing the Denmark star hoovering up silverware with his beloved side was the realisation of a fantasy for young Anders. 'I still get goosebumps thinking about it,' he said, of United's Treble-clinching victory over Bayern Munich in Barcelona.

'Peter Schmeichel was the hero of my life,' he said. 'I was Peter Schmeichel when I was playing in my parents' garden. I was always imagining that I was Peter at Old Trafford. He is the biggest goal-keeping legend at the club along with Edwin van der Sar.'

Born in a small town in central Denmark, Anders played for local side Odense Boldklub before a loan move to Norway's Aalesunds FK, which subsequently became a permanent deal that provided him with the platform to showcase his talents on the senior stage. After winning the Norwegian Cup in his first full season and duly being crowned the best goalkeeper in Norway, Lindegaard came to prominence at a time when United were looking for long-term reinforcements in the goalkeeping department, not least with van der Sar's retirement looming large.

The Reds' then reserve-team manager, Ole Gunnar Solskjaer, was alerted to Anders' potential and scouted him on several occasions before recommending that Sir Alex Ferguson move to bring the Danish international to Old Trafford. Amid a whirlwind of speculation that he could be joining his boyhood team, Lindegaard conceded that he was smitten with the idea of the move.

'United is the biggest club in the world and when they look at new players for new positions, basically they can pick whoever they want, so they probably have a list of hundreds of players,' he said. 'In the beginning, obviously, it was a big thing in my head and it took a lot of energy. When I turned off the light at night, I was lying in my bed, looking up at the roof with my eyes just wide open, couldn't sleep, just thinking, thinking, thinking.'

The move was confirmed upon the January 2011 transfer

window opening, when Anders admitted: 'Obviously it's the biggest dream of my life coming true. My father taught me to support Manchester United and it has been my dream since I was four to represent this club weekend after weekend in goal. I am not here just to be here. I am here because I want to be the best. This is the place where you can be the best and be respected as such.'

Despite Lindegaard's arrival, United continued to be linked with a string of other potential new signings to replace the departing van der Sar, but the Dane merely shrugged off the speculation. 'I am not thinking about Edwin's situation,' he stressed. 'I only focus on things I can do something about; that is me. I am completely ignoring all the speculation and talk about other goalkeepers. I cannot do anything about that so I don't think about it. It won't help me to be thinking about what if this and what if that. I cannot do anything about it. That would ruin my focus. Being number one at United is a goal far out on the horizon. It is not something I think about when I go to sleep at night. The only thing I think about then is tomorrow's training. But it is always there on the horizon that reminds you of where you want to go and what you want to be.'

A vocal, confident presence in between the posts, Lindegaard impressed in his early outings for the Reds as Ferguson sought to give van der Sar timely rests to preserve his freshness for vital late-season games. At the same time, the new arrival was endeavouring to learn all he could during the Dutchman's final months as a player.

'I am trying to draw experience from him,' admitted Anders. 'Training with him has been good for me. First of all, he's a great man and a good person, plus he's a great goalkeeper. Every time he's in action it's about staying focused. I believe his biggest strength is his mentality. He's very calm, no matter what the score is or what time it is on the clock. He never makes mistakes and always makes the right choice. Being here is just a huge privilege. You have the chance to play with the best players in the world, work with the best manager, coaches and facilities. You have the fundamentals to do your job and become as good as you possibly can.'

Knee surgery curtailed Anders' first season in England, and by the time of his next senior outing, the Reds had parted with a substantial fee to bring in the highly rated David De Gea from Atlético Madrid. The young Spaniard's testing start to life in the Premier League prompted his occasional rotation with Lindegaard, and the Dane mustered 11 senior outings in his first full campaign with the Reds. Despite De Gea's steady acclimatisation, Lindegaard repeatedly insisted: 'I'm not just here to pick my nose,' underlining his determination to establish himself as van der Sar's full-time replacement.

There were further openings in the early months of the 2012-13 season, and Lindegaard made 13 starts in what would prove to be Ferguson's final term as manager. The Dane's ten Premier League outings were enough to earn him a winner's medal in the Reds' record-extending 20th title triumph, but that euphoria soon made way for uncertainty.

David Moyes's installation as Ferguson's replacement, and his decision to replace members of the long-serving backroom staff, meant a change of goalkeeper coach as Chris Woods replaced Eric Steele. Though Anders struggled to find playing time under the Moyes regime, he was full of only kind words for his new coach. 'Working with Chris has been fantastic,' he said. 'He is a world-class goalkeeping coach and, even though I am not playing, I can't imagine not enjoying training with him. Enjoying your training is a big part of helping to keep you ready when you're needed and I enjoy everything about what we do.

'It's very difficult to describe, but I must say first that I am very happy to be part of the squad at United. I enjoy the spirit among everyone and I feel very good physically. I just have to keep my head held high and wait for my chance. I want to help United do as well as possible by being ready and available at my highest level whenever I'm needed.'

Though the competition for one starting berth could easily have sparked an unhealthy rivalry between Lindegaard, De Gea and club's homegrown young stoppers, the Dane admits that there is quite the opposite culture on the training ground. 'There has always been a special bond between keepers anyway, but I must say I think what we have here is stronger than anything I've seen anywhere else,' he commented. 'I really enjoy working with David. He's a great guy. We are serious in our work when we need to be, but we also have a lot of fun together. As a footballer, you always want to help others and you always want to be helped and that's what the keepers do for each other.

'I remember when I was a kid having one of the older and more experienced goalkeepers I was working with taking me aside and saying, "Listen, you need to work on this and on this." He really helped me and it's something I've always thought of during my career and I want to be able to do the same for the young keepers. So I will always try to help and encourage them.'

The curtailment of Moyes's short reign at Old Trafford meant that Woods's time with the club was limited to just one season, before the arrival of Louis van Gaal brought well-renowned goalkeeper coach Frans Hoek – the man credited as van der Sar's mentor – to the club at the start of the 2014-15 term.

'I have heard a lot of good things and I am really excited to start working with him,' said Anders. 'You benefit from having a period of time with every goalkeeping coach and it was quite a short period that we had with Chris Woods. We really enjoyed that time with him. But just looking at Frans Hoek's results – and what he has done for different goalkeepers throughout his career – speaks for itself. Everyone would be excited about working with him.'

Having honed his trade under Woods and his predecessor Eric Steele, the arrival of one of the game's most renowned coaches will allow Anders to continue his education as he looks to realise his long-term dream of becoming a first-team fixture for his boyhood club.

16. MICHAEL CARRICK

Position: Midfielder
Born: 29 July 1981; Wallsend, England
Previous clubs: West Ham United, Swindon Town (loan), Birmingham City (loan), Tottenham Hotspur
Joined United: 31 July 2006
Debut: 23 August 2006 vs Charlton Athletic (A), Premier League
Honours: Premier League (2006-07, 2007-08, 2008-09, 2010-11, 2012-13), UEFA Champions League (2007-08), FIFA Club World Cup (2008), League Cup (2009-10), Community Shield (2007, 2008, 2010, 2011, 2013)

Few players have split opinion more in the modern game than Michael Carrick, the United maestro who is repeatedly overlooked by his country – despite being the cornerstone of a club that has won eight major honours during his illustrious eight-season Old Trafford career.

Beloved by his team-mates and respected by his opponents, the Wallsend boy remains a cult hero for many observers who enjoy the subtler details of the beautiful game. And yet, there is a long list of England managers who have not utilised this pass-master's talents – which is ironic, given the Three Lions' reputation for losing possession against more aggressive, technically imposing foes.

While United fans are expected to defend one of their own, those from Old Trafford are not alone in championing Carrick's cause. Indeed, one such supporter is Xabi Alonso, the former Liverpool and Real Madrid midfielder who is widely regarded as the finest mover of a football outside of Barcelona icons Xavi and Andres Iniesta, as well as our very own Paul Scholes. As a neutral to this debate, the

World Cup winner's opinion on England's failure on the international stage carries a lot of weight.

'Steven Gerrard is a great player – he inspires and leads, he is very capable of making players around him raise their game, but he also needs players alongside to bring the best out of him. I've missed a player like Michael Carrick in the England midfield, somebody who knows how to be in the right place at the right time. Gerrard gains a lot from having a player like Carrick as a partner, somebody who provides the back-up he needs to be free to bring his power to bear decisively in a game.'

Thankfully, England's loss has been United's gain since Carrick moved to Old Trafford in the summer of 2006, when he instantly inherited the iconic No.16 shirt that was previously worn by Roy Keane. But what does the man himself think about his critics? Is he enraged by the lack of acclaim, annoyed by his treatment from England or perhaps even irked by the managers who've dismissed him?

'To be honest, it doesn't really bother me,' Carrick answered in May 2013. 'Anybody that knows me will tell you that I am not one for shouting from the rooftops or promoting myself. I just play my football and I gauge my form on the manager here and his response. You can't please everyone, it is impossible. As a footballer, if you are going about your business doing things that other people from outside of the club want or expect you to do, then you are not going to be successful.'

As Carrick readily admits, a quietly efficient display in front of the defence rarely troubles the editors of *Match of the Day*, whose job is to cram 90 minutes of high-voltage Premier League action into a tidy ten-minute package that can be easily digested. As such, you should not expect praise if your performance is not highlighted on national television. But rather than pushing forward in search of a moment that would be beamed into the front rooms of houses across the nation, Michael is interested only in doing his job. 'That is what people want to see, players scoring and creating goals, that is the highlight of watching football,' he explained. 'But not everyone can do that. You have got to have positions and you have got to have a place in the team. We have got plenty of players here who can score goals and can produce miracles. I am happy to be the supplier for that.'

Carrick's former manager Sir Alex Ferguson – who signed him from Tottenham Hotspur – had his finger on the pulse when describing the midfielder's personality at the end of the 2012-13 season, a campaign that had seen Michael forge an outstanding partnership with Paul Scholes – somebody with whom he had much in common, both on and off the pitch.

'Michael is not a guy that seeks a lot of publicity,' Ferguson explained. 'He is a quiet lad. He goes about his life in a similar way to Scholes. It doesn't mean to say he is not recognised by us. You get players like that. Denis Irwin was much the same. He was not the type to trumpet his achievements. It is quite refreshing in the modern game that we have players who can rely on their ability, not by promoting or projecting themselves. Michael is mentally strong, too. He has a different personality to most players. That can be misread by a lot of people, thinking he has to be encouraged all the time. That is not the case.'

Carrick's talent was initially discovered while playing as an attacking midfielder or centre forward for Wallsend Boys Club and his performances there attracted the attention of his boyhood team Newcastle, as well as Middlesbrough and Sunderland. After all three shied away from committing to a deal, West Ham intervened and quickly snapped up his services on the advice of their North East scout. Harry Redknapp was at the Upton Park helm when Michael was signed, and he became part of a golden generation that featured Joe Cole, Frank Lampard and Rio Ferdinand. While his young teammates were obvious thoroughbreds, it took time for Carrick to prosper.

'Michael came down at an early age and was as skinny as a rake,'

Redknapp recalls. 'He had a terrific football brain even then, but absolutely no strength. He always knew what he was doing, but couldn't perform as he would like to on the pitch because he was so thin. Then he shot up in height in a matter of months. He went from five feet six inches to six feet one inch. He was like a beanpole and he had growing pains and problems with his knees. We had to wait for him to fill out.'

West Ham's patience paid off and Carrick inked professional forms in 1997. After winning the FA Youth Cup, he became an established first-team player in East London. A nomination for the 2000-01 PFA Young Player of the Year award was recognition of his excellent start in the senior ranks, though things went sour two seasons later when the Hammers were relegated from the Premier League. Despite an exodus of talent, Michael stayed to fight another day in the second flight and helped his team-mates reach the play-off final, only to lose to Crystal Palace at the Millennium Stadium in Cardiff. By this point, he had two choices: search out pastures new, or run the risk of stagnating. With only a year left on his contract, the club listened to offers and sold him to Tottenham in the summer.

Although initially unfavoured by Spurs boss Jacques Santini, Carrick found an ally in the Frenchman's replacement, Martin Jol, who was impressed by what he had seen. 'The first time I saw him on the training pitch I thought: "He'll be an England international,"' claimed Jol. 'Everyone could see it. He's one of the biggest talents in England. He's a complete midfielder – a skilful player and passer.'

Carrick enjoyed two successful seasons at White Hart Lane and scored two goals in 61 appearances, which helped Spurs finish ninth and then fifth in the Premier League. Despite just missing out on the Champions League qualification places during his second campaign in North London, Michael would soon make the step up to Europe's elite competition after United agreed a deal with Spurs to take him to the Theatre of Dreams. While rumours of the transfer had circulated for a few weeks, the Reds' interest was nothing new. 'Michael had been spotted by us before he was at West Ham,' explained former assistant manager Mike Phelan. 'But West Ham reacted quickly. We saw him play while he was young and always admired the talent he had, but the timing never fell right.'

Self-assured off the pitch, Carrick remained as composed on it while bedding into the team and quickly silenced any doubters with a string of accomplished displays. He became a fixture in Sir Alex Ferguson's all-conquering side of the late 2000s that claimed English, European and world titles at a canter, exporting his unique brand of under-stated football to a global audience while winning the respect of his captain, Nemanja Vidic. 'From the players' point of view, Michael is a very important player for us,' the Serbian said. 'He brings a lot of balance to the team – he's a link between defence and attack. Maybe he's not the most attractive footballer – he doesn't often do fancy tricks – but for our team he plays a key role. He takes up good positions so the defenders can always pass to him and he defends very well. He's a top player and has a lot of passion for the game.'

Fans at Old Trafford were always appreciative of his talents, but exterior recognition did not arrive until the 2012-13 season when a nomination for the PFA Player of the Year award followed a campaign that had yielded 36 appearances and one excellent solo goal at QPR. Even Arsene Wenger, manager of long-term rivals Arsenal, spoke positively about Carrick's value and even went on record to declare his vote had gone to the man from the North East.

'Carrick is a quality passer and he could play for Barcelona; he would be perfectly suited to their game,' the Gunners boss said. 'I would have chosen Carrick for this award as Robin [van Persie] won it last season with us. Michael has a good vision and is an intelligent player, and it is for what he has achieved in his whole career as well. It is this year or never for him, just because he is thirty-one and he has been exceptional for United. I think Carrick is an underrated player in England and sometimes not only should the goal scorer be rewarded but the real players at the heart of the game.'

True to form, Carrick was overlooked and the gong went to Tottenham winger Gareth Bale, who would shortly leave for Real Madrid and La Liga. Although personal awards still mean little to Michael, he was rightfully acknowledged by his team-mates at Old Trafford who voted him their Players' Player of the Year and Rio Ferdinand was quick to praise his flourishing friend. 'You wish players like that didn't have to go through their careers searching for accolades,' he said. 'You would like to think people would just give them out. That hasn't been the case with Michael, which is unfortunate. All the talk will always be about other players who maybe do a little bit more explosive things than Michael does. He is laid-back and plays at his own pace, so he always goes unnoticed. But he is valued highly by each member of our squad, don't worry about that.'

The 2013-14 season did not produce any more personal acclaim, of course, although it didn't for anybody associated with United following a chastening campaign under David Moyes that saw the Reds drop to seventh in the Premier League, finishing outside of the top four for the first time since 1991. Carrick's year went from bad to worse when he was subsequently omitted from Roy Hodgson's England squad for the World Cup in Brazil. Although hindsight suggests this was a blessing in disguise, it certainly didn't feel that way for the man who had long harboured dreams of representing the Three Lions on football's biggest stage.

Looking ahead, Carrick's future at United now rests in the hands of Louis van Gaal, a keen admirer of his talent and experience in midfield. During his official unveiling as Reds boss, the Dutchman was visibly irritated by news of an ankle injury that would force his pass-master to miss the opening ten weeks of the 2014-15 season, a blow that also ruled him out of the running for the vacant club captaincy position.

While Michael's injury undoubtedly played a part in the arrival of versatile Dutchman Daley Blind, fans can expect the seasoned No.16 to challenge for a starting place upon his return, safe in the knowledge that few players can blend experience and skill in such vast quantities.

17. DALEY BLIND

Position: Defender/midfielder
Born: 9 March 1990; Amsterdam, Netherlands
Previous club: Ajax, Groningen FC (loan)
Joined United: 1 September 2014
Debut: 14 September 2014 vs Queens Park Rangers (H), Premier League
Honours: None

Just 90 minutes into his Manchester United career, having debuted in the renascent 4-0 win over Queen Park Rangers in September 2014, Daley Blind had already endeared himself to the Reds supporters and earmarked himself as an unsung hero at Old Trafford.

Club-record signing Angel Di Maria was undoubtedly the star attraction during the welcomed return to form, scoring one goal and playing a role in three more for Ander Herrera, Wayne Rooney and Juan Mata. His Argentinian compatriot Marcos Rojo also produced a quietly efficient display at left-back, while Radamel Falcao's cameo was sound-tracked by the biggest ovation of a particularly jubilant afternoon at the Theatre of Dreams. However, Blind's beautifully understated performance suggested the Dutchman can become an influential cog in Louis van Gaal's improving machine.

Blind's quietly efficient contributions maintained United's rhythm, moving the ball with unerring ease. There was nothing flash – no back-heels or outside-of-the-boot through-balls. It was just touch and pass, then another touch and pass. It was beautiful in its simplicity and glorious to watch. The Dutchman showed his street smarts, too, by regularly breaking up QPR's sporadic counters with his impressive reading of the game, sniffing out danger before it had even arrived.

'I was really excited before the game,' the versatile Netherlands star told reporters after the final whistle. 'It was a really good debut which I really enjoyed and the fans were amazing. Everything has gone well for me so far. I had a good week of training and everyone has been really nice and open, and given me a great welcome. I felt at home straight away.'

Speaking in his post-match press conference, van Gaal was quick to praise his new recruit and explained just one of the reasons why he authorised the player's £14 million transfer from Ajax on deadline day. 'He is a player who can see situations in advance,' the boss outlined. 'He can always pass to the free player and when he doesn't have the ball, he knows when he has to press the opponent. That's a very good ability to have. I like him as a defensive midfielder, but he can also play in central defence or at left full-back. He can run for ninety minutes too and is always fit. That's another very good quality for a player.'

Blind's performance against Harry Redknapp's QPR team marked a fresh, exciting chapter in a career that has seen him climb the ladder of European football with great patience and persistence. Indeed, just a few years ago, United's new No.17 and current Dutch Player of the Year was in genuine danger of seeing his dream of playing professional football descend into a nightmare.

As the son of Ajax and Netherlands legend Danny Blind, it was not easy for Daley to carry the heavy weight of expectation that bore down on his slender shoulders and, as a young man, he appeared to struggle at first. Having ascended the ranks of the Dutch club's hugely respected youth academy, his first-team debut arrived in 2008 but unfortunately did not pave the way for a guaranteed spot in the senior team at the Amsterdam Arena. Instead, it led to him being loaned to Eredivisie side Groningen FC for one half of the 2009-10 season, making 19 appearances along the way.

However, despite impressing throughout his temporary stay at the Euroborg Stadium, Blind's return to Ajax was met by unfair criticism from a minority of supporters who felt his place in the first-team squad was indebted to the presence of his famous father, who was also the club's technical director. As third-choice left-back under the leadership of former Tottenham Hotspur boss Martin Jol, Daley was facing up to the realisation that he might have to leave the club he had joined as a seven-year-old. 'The public was not always kind to me, they are quite critical here,' he later admitted.

The turning point crucially arrived in the winter of 2010 with the appointment as manager of Ajax icon Frank de Boer, who quickly set about restoring the principles that yielded unprecedented success during the imperious reigns of Johan Cruyff and Louis van Gaal. He also took note of the potential that Blind is now exhibiting and retained his services as a left-back, which allowed him to flourish in the Dutch capital. The inconsistencies that had previously dogged him were eroded and, more importantly, his confidence was restored. 'I'm indebted to Frank de Boer,' Blind later proclaimed.

Having played a part in the title-winning heroics of the 2010-11 season, Blind stepped up his development by registering a total of 55 appearances in the two following campaigns as De Boer's rejuvenated team retained their Eredivisie crowns. During that period, Daley also sampled his first taste of Old Trafford under the floodlights, as Ajax secured a shock 2-1 win over United in the Europa League last-16, coming on as an 80th-minute substitute for team-mate Nicolas Lodeiro.

Although his impressive displays at left-back had already made Daley one of the most improved players in the Netherlands, his true reinvention was just around the corner. De Boer's objective was to dominate games through possession, using circulation football as a means to not only create goalscoring opportunities but also as a defensive weapon – much like Barcelona during the Pep Guardiola years. If you have the ball then the opposition can't harm you. This plan was aided by the emergence of Blind as an unerringly effective holding midfield player who would instigate Ajax's pressing game and dictate the tempo of their play.

The transformation was smoothed by Blind's football education at the Ajax academy and a childhood that had seen him regularly play in midfield. As fans observed, his energy and discipline quickly formed the foundation from which the rest of the side's panache was constructed. In the role, Blind was essentially a third centre-back and conductor rolled into one. 'What he does seems simple, but often that is the hardest of all,' De Boer said. 'If you can make the right decisions and stay calm under pressure at the top, that's very difficult, but Daley does those things very well.'

Blind's consistent performances throughout the 2013-14 season, in which a fourth Dutch title was won, earned him the club's Player of the Year award having already received a first Netherlands call-up during a friendly against Italy in February 2013. He retained his position in van Gaal's squad for the World Cup in Brazil and found himself in the spotlight almost immediately, after supplying the cross from which Robin van Persie executed a textbook diving header past Iker Casillas during Holland's shock 5-1 victory over reigning champions Spain. Daley went on to register seven appearances at the prestigious tournament and scored once against Brazil, as the Dutch finished third.

Van Gaal took over United in the days that followed the World Cup, famously claiming he did not need a holiday when tasked with such a mouth-watering job. With rumours of a move for Blind already circulating around the press, it was seemingly inevitable that Blind would join the revolution at the Theatre of Dreams. As such, fans were hardly caught off-guard when the transfer was eventually confirmed on transfer-deadline day, although the player himself was completely taken aback by his move to England. 'It's a little bit crazy,' he explained, just moments after signing a four-year contract. 'I was with Ajax from seven years old which feels like a whole lifetime. But I'm twenty-four now and I think it's a good move to make and a chance like this may never come again. Ajax gave me everything that I needed to be a player in the youth academy and then the first team and I'm really happy that I was there for such a long time, and it was they who helped me get here.'

One of the most influential factors behind van Gaal's decision to sign Blind was the player's ability to adapt to his philosophy, which requires players to be able to fill a number of roles within the team. This led to speculation about where the 24-year-old would play for United, a debate that his former manager De Boer joined: 'He started as a full-back but I think now he prefers to be a controlling midfielder. He'll have two or three options at United – either at wing-back or on the left in a central midfield pairing. For Daley it's a great transfer. He's been playing for Ajax since he was seven years old and now he can hopefully show his qualities at United. He'll have to get used to the rhythm of the league first, but he's a really quick thinker and nowadays that's very important.'

Netherlands legend Johan Cruyff also praised Blind's measured approach to reaching the platform he stands on today, claiming more emerging Dutch talents should look to hone their skills in their homeland before seeking a move abroad. 'Educated at Ajax, on loan to FC Groningen and improving step by step at Ajax to eventually gain a top transfer to Manchester United after the World Cup,' the Dutch football icon wrote in his column for *De Telegraaf.* 'But apparently, even a role model like Blind cannot prevent children to leave Ajax too early and move abroad.'

Looking forward, Dutch journalist Marcel van der Kraan believes

Blind has all of the attributes needed to become a success at Old Trafford and will prove his old doubters wrong once again. 'Daley has come to United with a few league titles and trophies under his arm, while he has also been crowned footballer of the year in the Netherlands for the first time in his life,' he explained. 'If he follows in the footsteps of his dad, Danny, then he will be a success at Manchester United.

'He is an absolute first-class player,' van der Kraan continued. 'He has played almost every position except goalkeeper and striker at Ajax. It is one of the great things about young players who come out of that youth system. They have had a great education, they are very skilful and I think this is why Louis van Gaal has gone for this particular player because he knows he gives him something that he needs. Players need to follow his philosophy, as he so often says. Of course, we have seen so many skilful players in the Dutch league and it is so different once they arrive in England. The only thing that speaks for Daley Blind is that we had these worries about him before the World Cup, because he was making his debut on the biggest stage, but he surprised us all.'

What is perhaps most exciting about Blind's arrival at Old Trafford is his willingness to learn and improve under the guidance of van Gaal, a manager whose teachings he is eager to absorb. 'He is very honest to everybody, he knows what he wants and he knows his philosophy,' Daley claims. 'He can bring that to the players and he can make a team with everybody. That is a good start if you want to work for each other. I have really learned a lot from van Gaal and I like working under him.

'I worked with Frank de Boer at Ajax and I think Ajax made me more the player I am now,' he continued. 'Of course, I was with van Gaal at the World Cup and he also helped me a lot. I have learned a lot from him and I hope to learn a lot more from him this season. I think he can make me a better player in terms of positioning, where to stand and tactics in games because midfield is an important position to play. I hope I can get better at it every day.'

Although Blind's United debut slipped under the radar in comparison to his more illustrious team-mates, fans left Old Trafford with a sense of things to come. Given the intelligence of match-going Reds, who love a hard worker, his unsung reputation could yet be short-lived.

18. ASHLEY YOUNG

Position: Winger/wing-back
Born: 9 July 1985; Stevenage, England
Previous clubs: Watford, Aston Villa
Joined United: 1 July 2011
Debut: 7 August 2011 vs Manchester City (N), Community Shield
Honours: Premier League (2012-13), Community Shield (2011)

In the summer of 2001, Ashley Young was rejected by Watford's youth academy and told he should look for another club. This was a particularly seismic blow for the 16-year-old, who had recently frustrated a careers advisor by insisting his only wish in life was to become a professional footballer. Although he did not know it at the time, this early bombshell that threatened to extinguish his dream would eventually provide the foundation on which his entire career would be built.

After crying from the initial trauma caused by the body blow, Young took stock at his family home in Stevenage and thought hard about the options that were ahead of him. In his mind these were threefold: find another club, take up an offer of playing part-time football at Vicarage Road or get a 'proper' job. As the England international now explains, his heart took him in only one direction.

'When you're on the YTS [Youth Training Scheme] and that day comes when you're going to be told if you'll be kept or let go it's horrible, particularly at such a young age,' said Ashley. 'It's one of those decisions that can make or break you. I'd been at Watford since I was ten years old and I remember going into the meeting not knowing what was going to be said. When they told me I wasn't going to be offered a full scholarship, my heart sank and it felt like the world had ended.

'But they turned round and said I could still come in part-time, train twice a week with the full-time boys and play at the weekend. It was up to me to go away and decide whether I wanted to continue at Watford or go to another club. I went back home that day and I don't think I moved from the chair all day, it was tough. Mum and Dad were trying to get my spirits up, but I was really upset. It took me a few days to think about it and I decided I wanted to stay – it had been the only the club I'd known. There were other clubs who wanted to take me, but I felt like I wanted to stay at Watford and prove to them that I was better than they thought. Prove that I would make it into the first team.'

Young's initial rejection was based on various fragments of his game that required improvement and, to help him, he was sent to train with the Hornets' Under-18s, an age-group that was two years above his natural level. This was a daunting test but the decision paid dividends and he was starting matches within a year. Another promotion to the Under-21s followed and, with the wind in his sails, Watford finally offered him a professional contract that was gratefully accepted. Although this period was a tumultuous time in his career, the positives outweighed one significant negative.

Having climbed the ladder at Vicarage Road, Young made a long-awaited first-team debut during a 3-1 win over Millwall in September 2003, when he scored as a second-half substitute before contributing two more goals in his next four appearances for Ray Lewington's side. A place in the team for the remainder of that season was cemented with great style and verve, before his impressive form earned him the club's Young Player of the Year award at the end of the 2004-05 campaign. Flying high and now living the dream, his 13 Championship goals would then help the Hornets earn promotion to the Premier League under new manager Aidy Boothroyd.

Watford struggled in the top flight and earned just one victory in 19 matches before the turn of the New Year. Nonetheless, Young continued to flourish and attracted the attention of Aston Villa, who eventually paid £8 million for his services in January 2007. While eyebrows were raised by the fee, new manager Martin O'Neill was adamant his signing would step his game up to another level.

'He has got enormous potential and I think he will fulfil that,' the Villa boss commented. 'Ashley is a really talented player. I have seen a lot of him and I am going to back my judgement. He is only a young fellow and it will be hard to put him under the sort of pressure where he is having to justifying himself from minute one, but overall I have no doubt at all he is good enough. I know his potential but it is different knowing the potential of a player and what they eventually go on to achieve. I believe he has the ability to go on and achieve things.'

O'Neill's judgement proved to be shrewd and Young soon became a star in the Midlands, where his excellent form on the wings contributed to three consecutive sixth-place finishes for the Villans. So impressive were Ashley's performances, his typically reserved Northern Irish manager would later describe him as 'world class', after winning the 2009 PFA Young Player of the Year award, a prize he claimed ahead of Jonny Evans and Rafael da Silva.

By the end of the 2010-11 season, in which contract talks stalled as Villa dropped down to ninth, it became abundantly clear that Young was seeking pastures new and Sir Alex Ferguson took full advantage, sanctioning a transfer and a five-year contract. Continuing a familiar theme in his career, Ashley was ready to tackle another challenge. 'There's a lot of competition for places at the club,' he acknowledged. 'If you are in the team there is always going to be someone biting away at your heels trying to get in. I know it is going to be a challenge, but I'm up for that challenge. It is a prospect I always looked at from being a child – to play for one of the biggest clubs in the world. I've got that opportunity now so I've just got to take it with two hands.'

Highlights of his debut season at Old Trafford included a superb double in United's 8-2 annihilation of Arsenal, as well as another brace during a 3-1 win at Tottenham Hotspur, though any personal glories were regrettably overwhelmed by the agonising manner in which rivals Manchester City claimed the title on goal difference with just seconds of the season left to play. But under Ferguson's instruction to harness the pain of that defeat – a technique Young had mastered long ago – the Reds bounced back and claimed the 2012-13 crown at a canter, allowing Sir Alex to bow out at the top. Incidentally, it was around this time that Ashley bumped into his aforementioned careers advisor.

'I saw her and asked if she remembered our meeting,' he recalled. 'She said she couldn't. We laughed and I said, "I bet you don't!" I'd always had that goal to make it though, that desire and drive. I'm always asked what I would have done if I wasn't a footballer and I can't answer it because that's all I knew I wanted to do.'

The highs of his first title winner's medal were unfortunately short lived as United struggled under the management of David Moyes, whose ill-fated reign at Old Trafford was littered with lows, leading to his eventual dismissal in late April. Despite Young making 30 appearances under the Scot, seven more than his previous campaign, he was not exempt from media speculation that his Reds career might also be over.

Rumours of a potential exit were only enhanced by the appointment of Netherlands boss Louis van Gaal, who was a long-term admirer of the 3-4-1-2 formation that helped Holland finish third at the World Cup in Brazil. The system crucially relies heavily on wingbacks that can fulfil roles in both attack and defence over the more traditional wide man. But in a show of great respect, the Dutchman

Robin van Persie comes up against a familiar foe in United's 4-0 win over Queens Park Rangers in September.

Ander Herrera is welcomed to the Aon Training Complex by Sir Bobby Charlton on his first day at the club, in June. The Spanish midfielder was soon impressing his new team-mates.

Darren Fletcher's comeback from career-threatening ulcerative colitis
was completed when Louis van Gaal named him club vice-captain.

Antonio Valencia's pace and power on the wing have always made him more than a
match for even the best defenders during his time with the Reds.

The popular Brazilian Anderson has had an injury-blighted time at Old Trafford, but at his best he can be a match for anyone in a midfield tussle.

Marouane Fellaini holds off former team-mate Leighton Baines during United's victory over Everton this season.

With United facing a major injury crisis in defence, Patrick McNair stepped up to make his debut against West Ham at the end of September and immediately showed his enormous potential.

Jesse Lingard was United's top scorer on the 2013 pre-season tour – here he is scoring against the A-League All-Stars in Sydney.

Marnick Vermijl made his debut against Newcastle United in the Capital One Cup in September 2012, helping the Reds through to the next round.

Saidy Janko is presented with the Denzil Haroun Reserve Team Player of the Year award by Nicky Butt after a fine campaign in 2013-14.

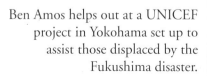

Tom Thorpe skippered United's 2011 FA Youth Cup-winning side, and he will be hoping to follow in the club's long tradition of building from within.

Ben Amos helps out at a UNICEF project in Yokohama set up to assist those displaced by the Fukushima disaster.

Never having scored for United at any level, Reece James whirls away in celebration after scoring on his senior debut in the pre-season tour of the United States. He was soon to notch a second.

Another product of the club's youth system, Tyler Blackett was a regular in United's defence at the start of the 2014-15 season.

The 'Iniesta-like' Belgian midfielder Andreas Pereira in action against Real Sociedad during a UEFA Youth League game in November 2013.

Will Keane arrives at Ann Arbor in Michigan ahead of United's record-breaking friendly against Real Madrid during this summer's pre-season tour.

A dream senior debut for James Wilson resulted in two goals in a 3-1 win over Hull City.

Goalkeeper Sam Johnstone found there weren't too many players rushing to take on this particular photo opportunity during United's pre-season tour of South Africa in 2012.

Assistant coach Albert Stuivenberg makes a point to Jonny Evans during the summer tour of the United States.

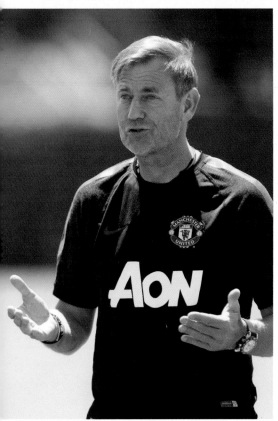

Frans Hoek made his reputation as a goalkeeping coach with his work with Edwin van der Sar.

Opposition scout Marcel Bout plays a crucial role in Louis van Gaal's backroom team. He's obviously just provided Wayne Rooney with a key insight into how to break down that week's opposition defence.

gave every player an opportunity to impress during the club's pre-season tour of America and was pleased by Young's willingness to adapt to his philosophy. True to reputation, the former Ajax boss also had a plan for the improving England international.

'He talked to everyone individually in terms of the positions he wants us to play and he spoke to me about more of the work I'd need to do as a wing-back,' Young revealed. 'It's a new position for me to be involved in. There are times when I'm running across the back-line and then I'm down the other end putting a cross in or going one versus one. There is a lot more running, but I think I'm capable of playing that position and the manager has thankfully shown faith in me by playing me there.

'I think football is all about thinking,' Young continues. 'If you've got a good football brain then you can play in many different positions and, luckily for me, I can play right across midfield and up front. In the new system you've got to have that awareness and that football brain to know where to be and what position to be in, and when to make the right runs to go back and defend. It also depends on the different formations other teams play against us. So there is a lot of thinking to do and you have to take a lot on board, but I think it's something I've adapted well to.'

Having shown his adeptness on tour by registering four goals and a Man-of-the-Match display against Real Madrid, van Gaal entrusted Young to fulfil the left wing-back role throughout all three of United's Premier League fixtures in August. His enthusiasm and versatility ensured that, contrary to rumours in the media, he remained a United player beyond the end of the summer's transfer window.

While a place in the manager's starting XI is far from guaranteed – with new signings Luke Shaw, Marcos Rojo and Daley Blind all inclined towards the left flank – Young has already displayed an admirable determination that could yet make him an influential player at the Theatre of Dreams.

With memories of his rejection at Watford still fresh in the mind, he knows where to seek inspiration if and when adversity comes his way. 'When I look at decisions that are made throughout life, I always think back to that day and how I was feeling – and how I managed to bounce back,' he said. 'That set me up for the rest of my career and I haven't looked back since that day. I've always been forward thinking and concentrated on wanting to improve and get better.'

20. ROBIN VAN PERSIE

Position: Striker
Born: 6 August 1983; Rotterdam, Netherlands
Previous clubs: Feyenoord, Arsenal
Joined United: 17 August 2012
Debut: 20 August 2012 vs Everton (A), Premier League
Honours: Premier League (2012-13), Community Shield (2013)

With a sculptor for a father and a painter for a mother, it is hardly surprising that Robin van Persie wields a creative mind that continues to fuel his lifelong fascination with the art of football. His only wish is to express himself in the game that dominated his childhood in Rotterdam, where he would often sleep with a ball under his quilt while dreaming of a professional career in the game. Even today, on the other side of 30, he speaks with an animated enthusiasm that is completely infectious.

While his parents succeeded in instilling a sense of creativity in their son, he does not share their love of the arts. Indeed, place a paintbrush in Robin's hand and you'll waste a perfectly good canvas. Football is his art.

'I don't see things the way my parents do,' van Persie explained. 'They can look at a tree and see something amazing, whereas I just see a tree. That's not to say I don't appreciate its beauty. When I watch the sea in somewhere like Sardinia, I see the beauty in that. But I think there is a creative connection with my parents. It's hard to explain in words, hard to put my finger on it.

'Football is where my creativity comes out. Like them, I think I see things other people – and other players – don't when it comes to certain situations. When I look at a football pitch I suppose I see it as my canvas. I see solutions, possibilities and the space to express myself. I am always looking for ways to be creative, to gain an edge. I wasn't artistic in drawing or painting, but I think I am artistic in sport. I think I'm always looking for the ultimate, the maximum. It's a challenge that excites me.'

His father Bob intuited from the outset that Robin was destined for great deeds in the world of football, not only due to his innate natural talent but also because a fortune-teller had imparted that very message during a chance meeting in an art gallery. 'When he was born, a clairvoyant told me what was going to happen with him,' van Persie Snr told the *Telegraph*. 'She told me that he would be in the Dutch national team, that he would be a king on the field.'

Despite this bold prediction, Bob is also adamant that he never pushed his son to follow football, and gave him options. 'If he had wanted to be a ballet dancer, it would have been fine with me. Anything he wanted to do. He was a difficult boy, overactive. When my wife and I divorced [Robin was five], he came to live with me until he was in his twenties. Until he turned twelve, I had a hard time controlling him. But suddenly he turned positive. He found football as something to put his energy into.'

Robin's mother, José Ras, moved to Zeeland near the Belgian border after splitting from Bob and now designs jewellery. She seldom speaks about her son's garlanded career, choosing to live a quiet life instead, but accepts his childhood habits meant it was almost inevitable. 'I expected him to do something with football on a professional basis, but I never expected it to be on this level. As a little boy he was always busy with the ball, and you could see he was fascinated by it.

'By five he could already control the ball miraculously. You could see he had a passion and the older he was, the more passionate he became. I always supported him and his two sisters in what they wanted to do. It is very important for the kids to do what they like so they can be happy. If their heart goes out to football, then that is what they should do. I tried to encourage them to develop their talent – and Robin's talent, obviously, was football.'

At 13 years old, van Persie joined boyhood team Feyenoord, a top club with a professional training set-up that would develop his potential. After a couple of years he had emerged as a prime talent and, on 3 February 2002, he made his much-anticipated debut for the first team. A few months later, he started on the left-wing in the club's UEFA Cup final victory over Borussia Dortmund.

All was going well and Robin was an instant hit among the fans. But it started to go wrong when he began to regularly clash with manager Bert van Marwijk, as well as senior pros Paul Bosvelt and Pierre van Hooijdonk – who famously took offence in a match against RKC, when van Persie pushed his older team-mate away to take a free-kick that forced an excellent save from the goalkeeper. Van Hooijdonk was still furious, as was his coach. Young players were told to be quiet and know their place at the club, but the new kid was not having it and left for Arsenal at the end of the 2003-04 campaign, excited by an environment where he could express himself without fear of reproach.

'It was my dream to play my whole career at Feyenoord,' Robin said later. 'I grew up in Rotterdam. It was my club. It was my dream, but things changed there and I learned a lot from the experience. It was quite difficult making that transition from the youth team to the senior team. Coming through the ranks, at fifteen, sixteen and seventeen, I was just playing with my friends. Then I'm playing with these adults. Some of them were thirty-three or thirty-four and playing for the last money they are going to make in their careers.

'I remember playing against PSV Eindhoven in the UEFA Cup when I did this trick and one of the older guys screamed at me, "Don't do that again. You are playing with my money!" I couldn't believe it because, for me, football had only ever been about enjoying myself. I wanted to win, of course, but if I tried a trick it was because I was trying to find a solution.

'I probably didn't respond too well to that kind of thing. I guess everyone makes mistakes. At the same time, though, some of the players at Feyenoord wouldn't show me respect because of the age I was, because I was just a kid. And I didn't think that was right.'

Van Persie was in his element under the tutelage of Arsene Wenger, a manager famed for polishing rough diamonds, and in hindsight, the Dutchman accepts the decision to move away from his homeland was pivotal in his career. 'Coming to England was the best thing that could happen, because I was taking myself out of my comfort zone, out of my nice warm city where I had my family and my friends, where everything was in place. Suddenly you are in a different country, you are lonely and you deal with it. It made me tough, it made me harder and made me more focused on achieving all my goals. It made me realise that I had the biggest influence on my career and no one else.'

While plying his trade at Highbury, before its Emirates Stadium replacement was built, van Persie also benefited from befriending two like-minded artists of the beautiful game in the forms of Gunners legends Thierry Henry and Dennis Bergkamp. The opportunity to learn from such maestros yielded obvious benefits for Robin, who was keen to soak up every lesson on offer.

'I had some really interesting conversations with Dennis and Thierry about football. It was fascinating to discover how they think about the game, realise how clever they were as players,' van Persie said. 'They were always one or two steps ahead of the defenders, which is especially difficult in English football. I also loved the fact they demanded such high standards and Thierry could be very demanding. He could never understand why a player would give him a bad pass and he would give them that look. The player would often respond by telling him he was trying to do his best. But I liked that about Thierry, because he raised the standard of the football. He demanded that we try and play to the highest possible level. Dennis was the same, just amazing to work with.'

Another positive influence on van Persie's attitude to football was Marco van Basten, the legendary Dutch striker who managed the national team between 2004 and 2008. It was his simple view of football that honed Robin's perception of his own performance, inspiring him to ask more of himself. 'He was a very special character, a very special man and he made me aware of what it was about,' United's No.20 explained. 'The way he looked at football was very cold, it was ice cold. It was just: in football you have to win, whatever it takes. As a striker you have to score and make your team win.

'I remember we [Arsenal] had played Manchester City and I hit the bar once, the post twice and one chance went just by it. We lost that game. So I went to Holland to play for van Basten and he asked me: "How was your game?" I said it was actually not bad, I was a bit unlucky but I think I played well because I hit the post twice and the bar. He then said: "Okay, you feel not bad? No, no! Robin, it's not good enough." He was straightaway putting it to me and said: "You need to make sure that you score those goals and that they don't go into the post or the bar. You should not be happy if it hits the bar or the post, because the bar or the post is not a goal. So no, it was not good. I watched the whole game. You've got to change your mentality of looking at football and those situations."

'He just opened my mind a little bit because he was right. It is about scoring a goal. Basically, the way he made me think about football is: anything else except a goal, except a win, is not good enough. So that was a good lesson for me at that stage of my career.'

In the summer of 2012, having listened to his 'inner child', van Persie left Arsenal and signed for United in pursuit of his first Premier League title. The decision was vindicated just nine months later when Sir Alex Ferguson's men secured the crown at a canter, with the Dutchman scoring 30 goals in a breathless season that left fans gasping for more. Unfortunately, the following campaign could not live up to such heady standards as the team as a whole struggled under David Moyes, while Robin could only register 28 appearances during an injury-hit term.

Van Persie's hopes of regaining his top form during the 2014-15 season were aided by the appointment of Louis van Gaal, a long-term ally following their success with the Dutch national team. Perhaps most importantly, they share a football philosophy and agree on how the game should be played, which augurs well for Reds supporters.

'We've had many great conversations over the past two years about football but also about other things,' said the striker. 'You don't have that bond with every coach. He has a different approach to the other coaches I've worked under, but I like it a lot. He is very clear and honest – he says when something is good and when something is not good, but there is always room for discussion. He creates a very relaxed atmosphere, but he is typically Dutch. Direct. Boom. He has only one aim, and that is to improve. I don't find that exhausting – I find it energising. It is wonderful.'

While van Persie is admittedly delighted with how things are shaping up at the Theatre of Dreams, with a talismanic new manager and a host of expensive new signings, his biggest hope is to retain that childish love of football that was nurtured at home in Rotterdam.

'My most important dream is to stay as long as possible the kid that I still feel within me,' he said. 'That's what I am. And that is what I always want to be: just a kid with only one wish, to play football.'

21. ANDER HERRERA

Position: Midfielder
Born: 14 August 1989; Bilbao, Spain
Previous clubs: Real Zaragoza, Athletic Club
Joined United: 26 June 2014
Debut: 16 August 2014 vs Swansea City (H), Premier League
Honours: None

A brave, intelligent playmaker who embraces responsibility and exudes aggression in the tackle: that is Ander Herrera, who became the first signing of the Louis van Gaal era upon joining United from Athletic Club in June. Thankfully, for Reds supporters at least, the 24-year-old Spaniard wields an appetite for adversity and rarely turns the other cheek. Despite his tender years, and his boyish looks, this fledgling midfield talent has plenty of experience under his belt and is not fazed by the challenge of bringing bite and creativity to United's engine room.

Although born in Bilbao, an inherently passionate district of the Basque country, Ander spent his formative years in Zaragoza and received his football education at Real Zaragoza. Having ascended the youth ranks, and through the B team, a first-team debut was made in February 2009 during a 1-1 draw with Real Sociedad. The then 19-year-old went on to register 17 appearances that season, helping his team-mates secure promotion from the Segunda Division. Ander's La Liga bow duly arrived on 29 August in a 1-0 win over Tenerife, when he replaced former Premier League regular Jermaine Pennant in midfield. That opening-day victory would eventually prove crucial as Los Blanquillos avoided relegation by just five points. The following campaign produced another 33 outings as new manager Javier Aguirre earned a 13th-place finish.

Herrera was notably transferred to Athletic Bilbao in the summer of 2011, which was a bold move considering his dad, Pedro, once played for Zaragoza and had also been their longest-serving sports director. It was a big deal, a genuine repatriation and the Basque club were understandably excited. It was also here, at San Mames, where Ander forged a fruitful relationship with Marcelo Bielsa, the maverick Argentine coach whose attention to detail brought results from United's new recruit.

'He's the most original, different, singular person that I've ever met,' Herrera explained. 'He's got an amazing mind. He has an incredible intellectual capacity for football. Nothing is ever left to chance; everything is studied to the finest details. He knows what every player can and can't do. He makes sure that everyone is on their toes. I've seen him speaking to the groundsman for forty-five minutes. I'm sure he would have studied grounds-keeping before that chat.

'Bielsa demands of others what he demands of himself. I've never seen a coaching staff work as hard as with him. He'd go crazy if a pole was half a metre the wrong way. I once had my feet on a chair. He came up to me and kicked the chair away. "Do you see me with my feet up?" he asked. You've really got to like football a lot to put up with him. I'm lucky as I love football. I watch videos. Others just like to play and they really suffer under Bielsa. I spent two years with him and I was always in the starting XI. I'm thankful to him, but I really enjoyed my days off.'

Herrera's first year with Bilbao brought him to Old Trafford as his team-mates faced United in the Europa League, a competition that Sir Alex Ferguson's men were forced to enter after exiting the Champions League at the group stage. The Reds were caught completely off-guard by the quality of Athletic, whose energetic approach bagged an impressive 3-2 win, with Herrera providing an assist for Oscar de Marcos. As Ander recalls, his unfancied team-mates arrived at the Theatre of Dreams with a simple plan: to have fun.

'We were under no pressure. Nobody expected us to win. Then I saw our six thousand fans and we all changed a little. That was the best game I've played. We were winning two-one and Bielsa would not let us stop. We thought he wanted to close down the game. No, Bielsa wanted a third and a fourth. He could live with conceding a goal from a counter-attack because that meant we'd have been attacking. He's a football romantic, Bielsa. He thinks that football should be a spectacle.'

A 2-1 victory in the second leg wrapped up a frighteningly straightforward aggregate win and, having witnessed United's downfall, Sir Alex was typically gracious in defeat and reserved special words of praise for the opposition. 'Athletic Club's work-rate is higher than any I have seen in Europe,' he told reporters. 'But it is not just about their work-rate, they are all very good footballers, too. They will go far in this competition and I wish them well.'

The Scot's assessment was proven accurate as Herrera and co progressed to the final in Bucharest, where they would lose 3-0 to David De Gea's Atlético Madrid. By this point, Bielsa's team had captured the attention of Europe's elite and big names were soon en route to pastures new. But not Herrera, who stayed to fight another day.

Before then, however, international duties came calling and Ander claimed silverware for the first time in his fledgling career – the UEFA Under-21 Championship. While representing his homeland in Denmark, he would notably make friends with recent opponent De Gea and fellow midfielder Juan Mata, two men he would meet again in entirely different circumstances.

Back at home, Bielsa continued to train his players into the ground while demanding gargantuan efforts on matchday. According to Graham Hunter, Spanish expert and acclaimed author, the Argentine's approach stunted Herrera's growth and delayed his expected promotion within the Spanish national teams. 'Bielsa was asking Ander to do too much physically when he had a minor injury,' said the Scot. 'Bielsa's side lost the Spanish Cup final three-nil and the

Europa League final three-nil because they were dead on their feet. Ander exacerbated a groin injury – after blossoming, winning the Under-21 final with Spain and reaching two finals with Athletic, there was a slight slowdown because of a groin problem that wasn't operated upon. It put the brakes on him becoming an automatic choice as Spain's central midfielder.'

The same injury would limit Herrera to just two goals and 32 appearances during the frustrating 2012-13 season, in which Bilbao slumped to a 12th-place finish in La Liga. The board opted not to renew Bielsa's contract and quickly hired Ernesto Valverde, whose first job was to fend off United's widely reported interest in his prized asset. Though a deadline-day bid was submitted, the move fell through and newly installed Reds manager David Moyes had missed out on his man.

Despite his disappointment, Herrera held a news conference and quickly put the matter to bed, before enjoying a hugely successful campaign that saw Athletic return to the Champions League via a fourth-place finish in La Liga. Having briefly played behind the main striker, he excelled as one of two organising midfielders in front of the defence, driving forward and dictating play. In fact, Herrera ranked among the top four players in La Liga for successful through-balls, behind Cesc Fabregas and Isco but level with his idol Andres Iniesta. Given the teams they played for, his numbers were perhaps even more impressive. Once again, as you would expect, his form did not go unnoticed.

On 26 June 2014, after another change of management at Old Trafford, the club returned for a second bite at the apple and finally ended months of speculation. Herrera duly signed on the dotted line to become an official Manchester United player, and the first new signing of the van Gaal era. While the Spaniard's interest in joining the Reds was well documented, the prospect of working under his new boss appeared crucial.

'The attraction of playing for and learning under van Gaal is vastly important for Ander,' claimed Hunter, who knows the player well. 'He has precisely the kind of intelligent, ordered, technical midfield industry which can lend itself to either the four-three-three which United are likely to enjoy, or the three-five-two with which Holland undressed Spain at the World Cup. Herrera helped his club reach the Champions League. Think what it means for someone from Bilbao to take the team to Europe's elite competition in a brand-new stadium, only to join United at a time when they won't be playing European football. That's how persuasive the van Gaal factor is.'

Another influence behind Herrera's decision was undoubtedly the chance to play alongside De Gea and Mata, his former international team-mates who would roll out the welcome mat upon his arrival in M16. 'I am very happy and very proud to be at Manchester United, I can promise the fans I will be a good professional and work hard,' Ander explained, having scribbled ink across a four-year contract that will keep him at Old Trafford until June 2018. 'I know David and Juan are very happy. I was talking to them, they told me that this is the biggest club in the world and that we have a very good squad. We are very good friends and I am sure they will help me to adapt and get to know the club.'

Michael Carrick, United's long-serving midfield architect, was also delighted by his new team-mate's arrival, having taken note of his quality during the Reds' aforementioned chasings against Athletic Club in 2012. 'I've played against him and he's a terrific player,' the Reds veteran said. 'The more quality you have, the better. He is certainly right up there. I'm sure he's looking forward to starting, getting the first game under his belt and fitting in. We'll certainly make him feel as welcome as we can.'

Ander's integration was hastened by his near-perfect command of English. He is highly intelligent and extremely articulate, having studied journalism until the age of 19, but a career in the Old Trafford press box can wait. In the meantime, his acumen translates seamlessly to matters on the pitch, even if there must be some concessions made as Herrera adjusts to the Premier League.

'It would be naive not to point out that it's a big change from La Liga in many different ways,' said Hunter. 'Even though he speaks English it's a big culture change. If anybody is expecting him to take the Premier League and United by the scruff of the neck from day one, that is unfair to ask of a guy at a club which didn't make European football last season, which is being reshaped and which has got a new manager. But by November or December, United fans will be saying, "We absolutely see what the fuss is all about, we absolutely respect his technique, we absolutely respect his will to win and we're excited to have him here."'

24. DARREN FLETCHER

Born: 1 February 1984; Edinburgh, Scotland
Previous clubs: None
Joined United: 3 July 2000
Debut: 12 March 2003 vs FC Basel (H), Champions League
Honours: Premier League (2006-07, 2007-08, 2008-09, 2010-11, 2012-13), UEFA Champions League (2007-08), FIFA Club World Cup (2008), FA Cup (2003-04), League Cup (2009-10), Community Shield (2003, 2007, 2008, 2010)

Were there ever a footballer to embody the rewards of bloody-mindedness, valour and vigour, then Darren Fletcher is that man. With almost every step of his Manchester United career, the midfielder has met a sizeable hurdle. Yet, be it football bureaucracy, questionable officiating or a potentially life-threatening illness, the Scot has marched through every blockade along his career path.

Now the Reds' vice-captain under Louis van Gaal, Fletcher's tale is a triumph against the odds, but not for one second will he countenance a victim's mentality, preferring rather to speak of the 'fantastic honour' bestowed upon him by the United manager.

Incredibly, the appointment as vice-captain came just a year after undergoing surgery which not only saved his football career, but potentially his life. Three years of the Scot's career were decimated by ulcerative colitis, a debilitating bowel condition, but at no point did his faith waver. 'I always knew I'd be back,' he has repeatedly stressed, matter of factly. Patience is a virtue Fletcher has been displaying ever since he joined the Reds as an 11-year-old – five years later, he was lined up to make Premier League history as the division's youngest-ever player, but league rules prevented a 16-year-old on schoolboy forms from appearing in first-team football.

That was in May 2000, as Sir Alex Ferguson was foiled in his bid to give Fletcher his debut in the champions' season finale at Aston Villa. Through a variety of injuries, including a broken foot, it was almost a further three years before the youngster made his bow, in March 2003 against Basel in the Champions League. Fielded as a right-winger but a central midfielder by trade, the wiry young Scot comported himself well enough to convince Ferguson that he was up to further involvement, and in 2003-04 he made an impressive 35 senior outings, including a sensational display in the unforgettable FA Cup semi-final victory over Arsenal at Villa Park. He ended his first full season in the first team with an FA Cup winner's medal, having started the 3-0 stroll against Millwall in Cardiff, and going into the 2014-15 season he remains the only player on United's books to have won the competition with the Reds.

As an incredible athlete with sensational stamina – he was one of only a handful of players to have beaten the dreaded 'bleep test' in training – Fletcher was increasingly utilised alongside Roy Keane, with the onus on the youngster to do much of the veteran skipper's legwork. It was by no means an easy ride, but learning his trade alongside one of football's greatest midfielders was an invaluable education. When Keane departed in 2005, his young peer was expected to step up as a replacement, but was soon having to face another injury-enforced spell on the sidelines, starting just a week before the League Cup final victory over Wigan Athletic.

Over time, Fletcher developed a reputation as a player trusted by his manager to excel at destroying illustrious opposition in the fixture list's bigger games. Arsenal, Liverpool and Chelsea often encountered the Scot at his rampaging best, and he admitted: 'I love challenging myself against all the best players and a lot of them play in the Premiership. I watch how good they are, but when we play them I think to myself: "Right, I'm going to see how good you really are. Fabregas, Lampard and Gerrard, I'm going to get against you and see how you like it. And when you've not got the ball I'm still going to get about you and see how you like it. I'm going to ask you: Do you fancy it? Do you like getting kicked? Do you like the fact that I am going to be at you for the whole ninety minutes? As soon as you get the ball I am going to be in your face. You are not going to like it one bit. And when we have the ball I am going to run you into the corner and you're going to follow me. Are you ready for that? Because that's what's going to happen."

'I get excited before the big games and not a bit nervous. I dreamed about playing in these games as a kid, so I'm determined to make the most of them while I am there, determined to test myself to my full ability. I don't want to sound big-headed, but I've never come up against anyone who has torn me to shreds. The only time that has happened has been in training against Roy Keane and Paul Scholes. I do enjoy the big games, I really do.

'In my younger games, I would perhaps sit back in the so-called lesser games. I'd let the lads go and play while covering for them. But in the big games I'd come out wanting the ball all the time. I've had to learn to do that in every game, to do it week in, week out. I've made a conscious effort in the last couple of years to play every game as if it's my last. If I'm going to stay in the team, I believe I have to play like that. It has worked quite well for me. My whole goal is to win the game and put in a performance which keeps me in the team. There is huge competition for places at Manchester United and if I don't have that attitude then I'll not be in the team.'

That experience came after the particularly trying 2007-08 campaign, when Fletcher enjoyed better fortune with fitness, but found it difficult to dislodge new signings Owen Hargreaves and Anderson – plus existing first-teamers Paul Scholes and Michael Carrick – from the heart of the Reds' midfield. An unused substitute on the days United clinched both the Premier League and Champions League titles, it was with Double glory still fresh in the air that he broached the subject of leaving the club with Ferguson. Reassured and talked round by his manager, Fletcher penned a new contract at the start of the 2008-09 term in a deal Sir Alex termed 'the relief of the season'.

The injury-enforced absence of Hargreaves allowed Fletcher to impose himself as the team's hassling, harrying disruptor in midfield once again, but his growing importance to the United cause was painfully underlined by his absence from a second consecutive Champions League final, this time won by Pep Guardiola's Barcelona in Rome. Harshly dismissed during the Reds' semi-final stroll against Arsenal, Fletcher quickly acknowledged the irony: he would miss the final after a sterling season fuelled by a near-identical situation a year earlier.

Not that he sulked, of course. Rather, he redoubled his efforts and became an even more influential player by putting in the hard yards in the Carrington gym. Gone was the wispy, willowy youngster who shirked the weights; in his place, an unerringly dedicated pro who had mastered his body. Mick Clegg, United's then-strength and conditioning coach, urged Fletcher to follow the example set by one of his freshly departed colleagues. 'I worked with Darren since he was a teenager,' said Clegg. 'But he wasn't kicking on. I told him to look at Cristiano Ronaldo and the way he was utterly dedicated. He came into the gym every morning and after every training session. If Darren wanted to get the best out of himself, he'd have to match that. So he started on a plan and steadily worked harder and harder, and over time he got it right.

'Gym work is a very fine balance – few get it spot on. Darren learned the secret of striking the balance between what you do on the pitch and what you do in the gym. The only other player I've worked with who got it so spot on was Ronaldo. But Fletch's lifestyle is perfect. It's not just down to his training, diet, or being teetotal. He's got a nice wife, nice children, a good lifestyle and he is fulfilling his dreams by playing for United. It makes for a very motivated, happy guy who was successful in his work.'

Unfortunately for Darren, who by the end of the 2009-10 term had won his seventh major honour after succeeding in his first League Cup final, he would soon be made to battle even harder for his dreams. 'I had been dealing with it [ulcerative colitis] for a while, but it actually came back in 2010 and I thought that the medication I was taking would deal with the problem, like it had done in the past, but it just seemed to keep lingering on and the medication didn't seem to work,' he revealed. 'So I tried stronger medication, thinking that was going to work, but eventually my body wasn't responding to any of the treatments and I was struggling. My day-to-day life was a struggle; my release was training and games, when I didn't feel like I had ulcerative colitis. It was a strange coincidence that before training and games, and maybe within an hour afterwards it would be really bad and a struggle.

'It just seemed to be my release, so I just kept going, kept doing it and I wasn't willing to let it stop me playing football. I tried a lot of different things and ultimately surgery was my only option after a couple of years of trying to go through all the medications, rest and all the different things the doctors and surgeons had told me. There was a day where I had tried my last medication. There was nothing else left for me to try. I tried alternative medicines as well, lots of things, but it came down to the last dose of treatment and if that didn't work then I knew surgery was the only option. I'd been presented with the option of surgery before but didn't really want to go down that route until I'd exhausted all the other options. Eventually I had no choice, at which point it was easier to accept because that's what I needed to get myself right.'

Restricted to just 20 appearances across the course of the 2011-12 and 2012-13 seasons, Fletcher underwent major bowel surgery in the summer of 2013 with a view to permanently ending his illness. Sensationally, he returned to action four months later and declared himself back for good.

'I'm sat here now, without ulcerative colitis,' he grinned. 'It feels great. I always knew I would be back and I kept that belief and mindset. I've been ready, champing at the bit to get involved and play. I feel like I'm making up for lost time, to be perfectly honest. I always cherished the position I was in and people were saying: "You should just be happy to be back," but I never wanted to get in that mindset because I think it's a dangerous mindset to get into, where you just accept a level. I always feel that if you put caps on just being happy and settling for stuff, then you can never progress yourself, so I see it that I've got a lot of lost time to make up for. I want to add those years onto the end of my career. My body, my joints have had two years of rest, so can I add those onto the other side of my career? That's the challenge and that's my mindset.'

Fletcher's absence and comeback straddled the departure of Ferguson, as well as the brief reign of David Moyes, and the arrival of Louis van Gaal prompted another twist in the Scot's eventful career, as he was named vice-captain ahead of the 2014-15 term. 'Darren is a natural leader and will captain the team when Wayne isn't playing,' said the Dutchman, who added: 'Darren is a very experienced player and a very popular member of the dressing room.'

The dressing room has changed substantially after a flood of new arrivals and the departure of several highly decorated veterans, but Fletcher remains as a monument to a glorious chapter in the club's recent history. In an ultra-competitive squad heavily replenished with top talents, the Scot knows that there will be yet another fight ahead as he bids to become a first-team regular again under van Gaal – but Fletcher is no stranger to scraps; he's been a battler throughout his career.

25. ANTONIO VALENCIA

Position: Winger
Born: 4 August 1985; Lago Agrio, Ecuador
Previous clubs: El Nacional, Villarreal, Recreativo de Huelva (loan), Wigan
Joined United: 30 June 2009
United debut: 9 August 2009 vs Chelsea (N), Community Shield
Honours: Premier League (2010-11, 2012-13), League Cup (2009-10), Community Shield (2010, 2013)

Blending the power of a bulldozer with the acceleration of a motorcycle, Antonio Valencia is one of the most impressive physical specimens to have graced United's right flank. Initially signed as a right-winger in the aftermath of Cristiano Ronaldo's then world-record departure to Real Madrid, the Ecuadorian has demonstrated admirable versatility and team ethic in his Old Trafford career to date, repurposing himself as both a right-back and right wing-back whenever required by his managers.

On his day, Antonio is virtually unplayable. If defenders are quick enough to match him for pace – and most aren't – then they almost certainly aren't strong enough to cope with his brute force. Though his goals return was modest throughout his first five seasons with the Reds, Valencia's varied array of crossing has made him a fruitful supply line from the right flank. There have been highs and lows along the way, as well as some yo-yoing between shirt numbers. While Antonio's United tale has perhaps been unconventional, it is completely fitting. After all, his path to stardom was almost untrodden; trading the Amazon basin for the banks of the River Irwell.

Born in Lago Agrio near Nueva Loja, capital of the Sucumbíos Province of Ecuador's Amazon Region, Antonio and his five brothers would scour their city and its surrounding villages in search of glass bottles for their father's bottle deposit centre. He would also help his mother sell bags of fruit juice on matchdays outside the Estadio Carlos Vernaza, the local football stadium.

Initially spotted playing football with his friends by ex-player Pedro Perlaza, Antonio enrolled with local team Caribe Junior at the age of 14. So impressed was Perlaza with Valencia's attributes that he recommended the youngster to El Nacional, a local team keen on encouraging burgeoning talents. It was also the Ecuadorian Armed Forces' team, requiring Antonio to move to Quito.

The youngster's stint of national service and football training had a swift and lasting effect. 'Undoubtedly the work he did in the minor divisions with El Nacional helped him a lot to increase his strength and power,' says Ecuadorian football journalist, Rodolfo Mazur Oyola. 'El Nacional was the club that shaped him professionally. They honed his technique and also helped him in his personal training. He was always a special player due to his skills, but he used to be thin until he spent some time there. He began training with former members of the Ecuadorian national squad, who guided him and recommended he be taken to the first squad. It didn't take long for him to gain the attention of Luis Fernando Suarez, the coach of the national team.'

'When you're only fifteen years old and you leave your family behind to go to the capital and play for one of Ecuador's top sides, Nacional, it's a brilliant experience,' said Antonio. 'It was really great. I'd do it again without a shadow of a doubt, both for my family and for the club, Nacional.'

It would prove a whirlwind few months. Just 12 weeks after scoring twice on his international bow, and still only 19, Valencia was whisked to Villarreal by Chilean coach Manuel Pellegrini, later of Manchester City. In almost no time, the youngster had gone from Ecuador's second tier to Europe's top level, and a place on the bench when Villarreal held United to a goalless draw in the Champions League in September 2005. Playing time would prove elusive at El Madrigal, however, and he was sent out on loan to gain action at Recreativo de Huelva, in Spain's second flight.

Valencia recalled: 'Initially my big aim was to play for the national team and after that, who knew? To be totally honest, it hadn't crossed my mind to go over to Europe quite so soon, but God blessed me enough and I was able to make the big step of joining Villarreal for a year and that was it. I'd arrived in a country which didn't have the same customs as Ecuador, I'd left my family and everyone behind and I found myself somewhere where it was very cold, so I was a bit down in the dumps at first. I was there for six months and then went on to Recreativo de Huelva for another six months. I guess that time was fairly difficult, but thanks to God again because He had a good plan in mind for me, and I think He delivered everything that I really wanted.'

Though he had dropped a division, Valencia's displays in Recreativo's successful promotion push kept him in the frame for his country. Antonio was a cornerstone of Ecuador's World Cup qualifying campaign, and it was in the tournament proper in Germany where his career took another unlikely twist as he played his way into the attention of Wigan Athletic manager Paul Jewell. 'I went to watch Ecuador against Poland and this lad stood out, playing in central midfield,' Jewell said. 'I thought he was a good player and when I found out he was twenty I couldn't believe it. I watched him for the rest of the tournament, pursued it and we got Antonio on loan with a view to buying him. The daft thing is that there was no competition for him. I think he definitely slipped through the net of the big clubs. I was really impressed when I saw him because he had such a great understanding of the game.'

The language of football proved Jewell's most effective method of communication with his new signing, who had little knowledge of English and needed a dressing-room interpreter to convey tactics before matches. 'It was an even bigger culture shock than Spain,' said the winger, 'because when I arrived I saw that you drove on the other side of the road! It was quite difficult in those early months. If you leave your home to go anywhere it can be difficult, and I did find it really tough. But I gradually got used to things. It helped me a lot. I was fairly lightweight at the time, and I hadn't been used to doing gym work or much else on the physical side, so when I got to Wigan, I thought to myself that if I wanted to stay in the Premier League for some time, I needed to work hard in the gym, train and prepare well and eat the right food. Straight away things started to go better for me.'

Antonio made a mockery of linguistic difficulties with a swift integration to the Latics set-up. 'He was such an intelligent footballer that he just slotted in really quickly,' said Jewell. 'He's a very intelligent boy. He'd pick up on what I said, even though it was in a Scouse accent. Every day he worked hard, was very courteous, very tough and a terrific pro. As a manager you'd love a team of Antonio Valencias. He was suited to English football because he's tough. Not many players come over from Ecuador with a silver spoon in their mouths, and you could see immediately that he was a hard worker and he flourished. I see him now and he's at one of the top clubs in the world, which is no surprise to me because he's that good a player.'

The move had a knock-on effect back in Ecuador. 'The entire country was thrilled,' reveals Oyola. 'Without any doubt, his presence at Wigan increased the interest of the Premier League, which was already followed closely by many people. People wanted to follow his development. Unfortunately, because Wigan were a small team, their games were not broadcast regularly, so fans used to wait for the release of special reports in order to see how he did. However, when a Wigan match was announced to be broadcast, the whole country was there to see him in action, regardless of the time.'

It didn't take too long for Valencia's audiences to grow. Wigan exercised their option to sign the winger permanently from Villarreal in January 2008 – for a meagre £4 million fee – and a year on, Latics manager Steve Bruce revealed that Antonio had rejected the chance to join Real Madrid. Six months later, however, he couldn't resist the chance to be part of United's rebuilding exercise after the departure of Cristiano Ronaldo.

'I was on holiday when I heard that United were interested in me,' Valencia recalled. 'My agent told me we had to travel over here because they wanted to speak with me and I couldn't believe it. I can remember calling my mum and dad, we had a chat and they were delighted. They are moments that you are never going to forget. I think that as a young lad, I was so keen and so excited to play for the club, I didn't even look at the figures or anything. The only thing I wanted to do was put on the United shirt and play for the team, so the negotiations did not last very long. I remember being in Ecuador and being really nervous. It was Manchester, and I had to make sure I was good enough to be at United. I had to make sure I was fit and well prepared. When I arrived I was nervous, but I was with friends who loved me and rated my ability, and who told me to relax and that everything would turn out well.'

Valencia immediately struck up fruitful relationships with his new colleagues, and his arrival coincided with the most prolific season of Wayne Rooney's career – the striker was on course to double his previous season's tally before injury decimated the final eight weeks of the campaign. The form of his supply lines – Nani and Valencia – was central to his success.

Antonio's second season with the Reds failed to reach the levels of his first, but through no fault of his own. Having suffered a fractured and dislocated ankle in an early-season draw with Rangers, he missed six months of action. Despite a rapid recovery to finish the 2010-11 term in devastating form, Antonio found his start to 2011-12 similarly disrupted by both an ankle blow and a pressing need to operate as an auxiliary right-back. He played his way into form, however, and swept the board at the Reds' end-of-season awards, taking home Player of the Year awards from his peers and the supporters, as well as the Goal of the Season award for a thunderous effort at Blackburn.

Michael Owen's departure freed up the famed No.7 shirt, which Valencia duly inherited for the 2012-13 season. Yet, while he ended the campaign with his second Premier League winner's medal, he was unhappy with his form, feeling burdened by the pressure of the shirt, and reverted back to his No.25 after just one season. 'I think it turned out to be a very good number for me when I first arrived at the club as I was just given the number twenty-five more or less,' he explained.

'But things went really, really well. I played well wearing that shirt, so I think it was a decision I came to in the summer. Maybe if I can get back to the form I showed before, why not? It is a good idea to start wearing it again. It had been something I had been thinking about for quite a long time. I'd been considering a change back and maybe it is psychological or maybe it is just all about a good-luck symbol, if you like. We get a lot of that in Ecuador, maybe superstition, and l hope it continues and still brings me more good luck.'

Though Antonio conceded that he was frustrated by a lack of playing time under the management of David Moyes in 2013-14, his form did markedly improve on the previous term and the arrival of Louis van Gaal signalled better news for the Ecuadorian. The Dutchman's penchant for using wing-backs lent itself to Valencia's attacking instincts and defensive diligence, and his versatility should bring more minutes on the field. Patrice Evra once joked that he thought Antonio had eaten a motor, such was his energetic approach, and, even after taking a long and winding road to this point in his career, Valencia still has plenty left in the tank.

28. ANDERSON

Position: Midfielder
Born: 13 April 1988; Porto Alegre, Brazil
Previous clubs: Gremio, FC Porto, Fiorentina (loan)
Joined United: 1 July 2007
Debut: 1 September 2007 vs Sunderland (H), Premier League
Honours: Premier League (2007-08, 2008-09, 2010-11, 2012-13), UEFA Champions League (2007-08), FIFA Club World Cup (2008), League Cup (2008-09), Community Shield (2011, 2013)

An enduringly popular figure at the Aon Training Complex, Anderson has both enjoyed the highest highs and endured sapping lows during his eventful career at United. After bursting onto the scene as an unknown quantity in 2007-08, the skilful Brazilian midfielder ended his first campaign as a Champions League winner and looked set to become a fixture in the Reds' engine room, only for a succession of niggling injuries and fitness concerns to punctuate his career thereafter.

His energetic approach to life at United – allied to dominant displays against established opponents such as Steven Gerrard and Cesc

Fabregas – quickly endeared him to supporters, who remain desperate for him to succeed – as does the player himself. 'It's not just the fans who've been frustrated, I've been frustrated too,' he explained in August 2013. 'I never asked to be injured, I don't want to be injured. I want to play every week for Manchester United, I love being here.'

Anderson began his career at Gremio, who are one of two teams in the Brazilian city of Porto Alegre alongside fierce rivals Internacional. His breakthrough arrived in the 2003-04 season, when the cash-strapped club were forced to promote their best young players into their first-team squad. This led to Ando making his first-team debut during a 3-1 derby defeat to neighbours Inter. Despite the ferocity of the occasion, he wasn't fazed and scored a consolation strike from a free kick, though his emerging talent was not enough to prevent his side's eventual relegation from the top flight.

A year later, Gremio were back on form and booked a place in the play-off final against Nautico with promotion to the big time up for grabs. The match was incredibly tense and Ando's team-mates struggled to make an impact in front of 20,000 opposition fans, whose support increased when awarded a controversial penalty in the 75th minute, a decision disputed so fiercely that Gremio were reduced to just seven players for the last 15 minutes of the game. Incredibly, the penalty was saved and the ball was quickly sent upfield, where Anderson had spotted an opportunity to make his mark. He controlled the ball, ran past several defenders and scored the tie's winning goal. Gremio held on to their lead and were duly promoted. A film was later made about the game, which became known as the 'Battle of the Aflitos'. The result also had a profound effect on the city and half of Porto Alegre, a city of 2.5 million citizens, partied for days in the name of Anderson.

Having scored his famous goal, the Gremistas' cult hero had caught the attention of bigger fish and was quickly sold to Porto for

€7 million in January 2006. The 18-year-old continued to excel while plying his trade in Portugal and claimed two Primeira Liga titles, while also making his debut in the UEFA Champions League. Although his second season was disrupted by a broken leg, the charismatic Brazilian made a full recovery in time to complete his £21 million transfer to United in June 2007. 'I cannot wait to play in the same team as Cristiano Ronaldo, who is a great player, as well as Wayne Rooney and many more,' he explained upon arrival at Old Trafford. 'I could not imagine I would ever get to work with a manager like Sir Alex Ferguson, but it has happened. What can I say? It is a dream the size of the world.'

United's capture of Anderson was several years in the making and was teed up by ringing endorsements from Ferguson's former assistant manager Carlos Queiroz and his brother Martin, who was also the club's head scout. 'Carlos, through his Portuguese connections, told us there was a young boy at Porto from Brazil called Anderson,' Sir Alex revealed in his 2013 autobiography. 'He was 16 or 17, so we kept an eye on him. He was in and out of the team, a game here and an appearance from the bench there. Then he played against us in the Amsterdam tournament and I resolved to act, but the following week he broke his leg. When his recovery was complete, I sent Martin over to watch him in every game for four or five weeks. Martin said: "Alex, he's better than Rooney."' Based on this description, the former manager gave the go-ahead for David Gill to complete deals for him and Sporting Lisbon winger Nani on the same day.

Anderson impressed in his first season at Old Trafford when the samba star looked like the most promising player at the club. An almost completely unknown quantity, he arrived at the club as a support striker but was soon repurposed as a central midfielder, on account of his energetic surges and knack for carrying the ball forward at pace. His great intent and urgency, allied to an infectious personality, quickly made him a fans' favourite at Old Trafford, and his first term in Manchester could not have gone better. It was glorious to watch, but not as satisfying as seeing the 20-year-old's penalty sail past Chelsea's Petr Cech in the 2008 Champions League final shootout in Moscow. The following campaign would yield even more silverware as Ando helped the Reds lift the Club World Cup in Japan and the League Cup at Wembley, before collecting his second Premier League title winner's medal in May.

Since then, however, Anderson has failed to exceed 30 appearances in a single season as injury problems diminished his role towards the end of the Ferguson era. Shortly after the appointment of Sir Alex's successor, David Moyes, he spoke of a desire to succeed at Old Trafford. 'I miss my children who are in Porto Alegre, but I'm happy being here with my three dogs Wes, Dani and Catarina. The fans are nice to me, I have friends here. I'm serious about doing well. Maybe I joked too much in the past, tried to be the Brazilian player who was always joking, but I was young too. Now I am more serious, I've started to eat properly, to sleep properly. I have to look after myself if I'm going to be at my best for Manchester.'

Still a popular figure in the dressing room, his team-mate Rio Ferdinand was quick to support the Brazilian's positive thinking. 'I don't think his talent has ever been in doubt, but he's had a few injuries over the years,' explained the defender. 'If he gets a clean bill of health, who knows what he can do? He's different from any other player we've got. In today's game, if you have a player who can go past people in the middle of the park then it's a big commodity. Anderson can do that, but we've never been able to get that out of him on a consistent basis because of injuries. He's got the potential to do it. If he can stay fit this season then it will be almost like having a new signing.'

Despite such an admirable attitude, and the support of his friends, Ando's contribution was further reduced under the management of Moyes, who eventually granted his wish for first-team football. A short-term loan move to Fiorentina was approved for the second half of the 2013-14 campaign, a period in which he made seven appearances for the Serie A side before returning home to United, where former Netherlands boss Louis van Gaal had just taken hold of the managerial reins.

After missing out on the club's hugely successful tour of America with a groin injury, Anderson registered first-team outings during early-season matches in the Capital One Cup and Premier League, before surviving the deadline-day cull of players that saw several team-mates leave for pastures new. Unquestionably gifted, the Brazilian retains a special place in the affections of his colleagues and supporters, and will forever be known as a star of the Reds' unforgettable 2007-08 Double season.

31. MAROUANE FELLAINI

Position: Midfielder
Born: 22 November 1987; Etterbeek, Belgium
Previous clubs: Standard Liege, Everton
Joined United: 2 September 2013
Debut: 14 September 2013 vs Crystal Palace (H), Premier League
Honours: None

Almost every player who signs for Manchester United quickly stresses that they have realised a lifelong dream by joining an institution of the Reds' stature. That was no different for Marouane Fellaini upon his arrival at the club, even if his first campaign at Old Trafford hardly followed his fantasy.

Signed in the final seconds of the summer 2013 transfer window, the Belgian international suffered a serious wrist injury within a month which required surgery two months later, prompting a lengthy spell on the sidelines. When he did play, the wealth of creative options in his preferred position as an attacking midfielder meant a repurposing to an unfamiliar defensive midfield role and, to cap it all, David Moyes – the man who signed him for both Everton and United – left Old Trafford before Fellaini's first season was out.

Yet, the Belgian's fighting spirit was in evidence long before his move to United. His combative displays against the Reds were devastatingly effective and yielded three important goals for Moyes's Everton in head-to-head meetings, and Fellaini will knuckle down in order to prove his worth in Manchester.

'I need to be fit to be good,' he declared. 'Even when I am injured I can play but the fitness is not the same. I was injured for three months and that was a difficult moment for me. When you arrive in a new team you want to play, you want to stay with the team and when you can't play it is difficult to see the team – even off the pitch. I will look to show what I can do.'

Fellaini's attributes centre around a deep-rooted athleticism which could have led to a career as a long-distance runner. As a child growing up in Belgium, Marouane would run to school while his father, Abdellatif, cycled alongside him, holding a stopwatch. He would also partake in nightly training sessions spent trying to score past Fellaini senior, formerly a professional goalkeeper in his native Morocco.

'Had he not been a footballer, he could have been a runner,' Abdellatif declared. Football was always top of the agenda, however, and Marouane trialled with Anderlecht at the age of seven. A regular goalscorer even as a midfielder, Fellaini quickly became a hot property and moved regularly around Belgian football, from Mons to Royal Boussu Dour Borinage to Sporting Charleroi, before joining Standard Liege.

It was there that he made his senior debut, aged 18, and he was soon catching the attention of scouts. Already a Belgian Under-21 international – having chosen to represent them rather than Morocco – it was two years later, in 2008, that he was named the Juliper League's best player of African descent. Fellaini was snapped up as Everton's record signing and his country's most expensive player at the time.

He swiftly set about making an impression at the club's Finch Farm training ground. 'It was quite unusual, really,' recalled Toffees defender Leighton Baines. 'In his first week, he kept going around smashing into people with these wild tackles. Some of the lads wouldn't go near him. I think he just wanted to show that he shouldn't be taken lightly.'

That over-exuberance continued throughout a hectic debut season. He took just 17 Premier League appearances to amass ten bookings, but vowed to curb his undesirable habit and picked up just two more over the remainder of the 2008-09 term. At Everton's end-of-season awards, he was named the club's Young Player of the Season, and over the following four campaigns he underwent a striking evolution to become one of the division's outstanding central midfielders, repeatedly setting Everton's statistical benchmark for distances run, tackles made and passes completed.

'He became a really good player during his time at Everton,' says Greg O'Keeffe, the *Liverpool Echo*'s Everton correspondent. 'After five years at Goodison Park, he was ready to be challenging for honours every season. Fellaini is now a really interesting player. He is a very good number four, sitting in front of the defence, and he can be really influential in that position, breaking up attacks and bringing real presence into that area. But he can also do a great job in and around the opposing penalty area. It's the old "good feet for a big man" cliché, but he really has got loads of ability above and beyond just being a target man who's excellent in the air. He's sharp, intelligent and his goal return speaks volumes for his threat. You'd be hard-pressed to find a better professional – all his managers have said as much.'

So, when Moyes left Goodison Park for Old Trafford and found a United midfield in need of reinforcements, it was inevitable that

Fellaini would be a contender to fill the void. 'When David came he looked at the squad and thought one of the players we needed to bring in was someone with those physical attributes in the middle of midfield who could give us strength and aggression in certain games and maybe allow one or two of the others to play,' said former assistant manager Steve Round.

'That, coupled with his ability to score, made him feel that Marouane would be a really good acquisition for United. When you are building a squad to compete on all fronts you don't want every single player to be the same. You want options and differences. There are different permutations. It gave the manager options he didn't have before. Marouane is a lot better footballer than he gets credit for. His feet and his technique work are really good. He is aggressive and tackles. He also has great fitness stats. He is one of the highest runners in matches. He will regularly do over twelve kilometres a game and he can run, goodness me he can run. He was ready for the step up.'

Fellaini's late arrival meant that his start to the 2013-14 campaign was a fragmented affair, having featured in Everton's opening games while knowing that a transfer across the North-West could be on the cards. 'It was difficult because for two months I did the preparation with Everton and I didn't know if I would go or not,' he said. 'But in the end I wanted my transfer and I signed for Manchester United. It was a lot of stress but good in the end.

'I knew about United as a kid because I watched them on TV and I read football magazines. I remember watching the game against Bayern Munich in the Champions League final in 1999 so I knew all about the club. Roy Keane was an inspiring figure. Manchester United had a lot of great players and that is why they have won so many trophies. When I joined, I thought: "Wow, this is different!" It was very good at Everton, but this is different. Different atmosphere. Different club. Everything is different. It is good to see that. This is a very big team – the biggest team in the world. I feel I know the players now. I know the club. It has been a good experience to be training with Wayne Rooney and Robin van Persie. Patrice Evra explained a lot about the club, how the team plays, and how they have to win trophies.'

The Reds' failure to compete for silverware in Fellaini's debut campaign hastened the departure of Moyes, and the Belgian retains a fondness for his former manager. 'I learned a lot from him and for that I am very grateful – it is a shame it didn't work out for him,' he said. Some onlookers were quick to write off Fellaini after his injuries and mixed form contributed to only sporadic involvement through-out his first term at Old Trafford. Procured for a substantial fee, stationed in the centre of the park and standing at over six feet four inches, even before his mighty afro is taken into account, there was no hiding place for the conspicuous Belgian.

'I was United's only summer signing, so the media spotlight has been fully on me,' he conceded. 'I couldn't believe what I saw when I arrived at the club. It was a change and a big leap for me. I am not replacing anyone at United. I am Marouane Fellaini, not Paul Scholes or Michael Carrick, and I'm going to play my own game and be a success. I can make a real contribution to the team winning trophies in the future. It is a dream for anyone to play for Manchester United.'

Fellaini's confidence in his own abilities is backed up by a host of team-mates at club and international level. For Manchester City captain Vincent Kompany, Marouane's Belgium team-mate, it is only a matter of time before the real Fellaini steps forward and makes a sub-stantial impact at Old Trafford.

'People shouldn't forget that it was Fellaini's first season at Manchester United,' said the defender. 'It's a big move and he deserves some time. It will sound weird because he plays for the red half of the city, but I want him to get back to his best. He's one of those special players. You just feel he can have a big impact on the team. They will need him a lot. It's just a matter of time really because he's got the lot.'

The arrival of Louis van Gaal as United's manager ahead of the 2014-15 campaign provided an opportunity for every player to start over, regardless of what had gone before, and Fellaini was determined to take the opening. 'I want to fight for my place,' he insisted. 'The coach wants to play with the eleven players who make the best team; I want to be part of that. I always play for the team so when the manager says "play there" I will play there. I don't think about myself.

'I know we can win in one game against any team. But when you play for Man United you need to win every game. I have never won a trophy in England. I will work hard, the club will work hard, and the new staff will work hard to win trophies. As players we must take responsibility for our performances and it is up to us to help the new manager turn United back into a team capable of winning the title.'

Circumstances once again worked against Fellaini as he sought to impress van Gaal. Firstly, his role in Belgium's World Cup campaign ensured a late return to pre-season training. While a last-minute friendly winner against Valencia – his first goal for the club – did cap an impressive cameo at Old Trafford, Fellaini soon suffered an ankle injury which heavily disrupted his start to the season.

Given the chance to return to – and maintain – full fitness, the Belgian does provide different options to a midfield roster now lavishly replenished with Ander Herrera and Daley Blind, in addition to the existing ranks. Fellaini's effectiveness as a central coagulant, his physical presence and versatility in midfield and as a makeshift support striker, render him an adaptable weapon with genuine value to the United cause. Given time and an upturn in fortune, there is still time for Fellaini's Old Trafford dream to come true.

33. PADDY MCNAIR

Position: Defender
Born: 27 April 1995; Ballyclare, Northern Ireland

Previous clubs: None
Joined United: 1 July 2011
Debut: 27 September 2014 vs West Ham United (H), Premier League
Honours: None

For every young player at Manchester United, the plan is simple: break into the first team, retain your place and continue the club's rich history of promoting from within. Doing so is never easy but, with a manager like Louis van Gaal at the helm, such lofty ambitions have become much more achievable.

Paddy McNair is a perfect example of somebody who claimed his opportunity with both hands after producing an ice-cool performance during September 2014's 2-1 win over West Ham, becoming the sixth Academy graduate to play under the former Ajax boss in the opening six games of 2014-15. The Northern Irishman was also credited for salvaging three points, having executed an intelligently angled header away from goal late on to prevent a certain leveller for Hammers striker Enner Valencia.

Although McNair was admittedly plucked from (relative) obscurity to fill a defensive void left by injuries to Phil Jones, Chris Smalling and Jonny Evans, plus a suspension for Tyler Blackett, he will not have cared one bit. He's now on the manager's radar, which bodes tremendously well for the future.

'He played very well,' van Gaal explained. 'I could have imagined a performance like this before the match because he's a very good player. Mostly, players like this have good debuts. I'm very pleased for him that we won, because he played very well and his goal-saving header in the second half was fantastic. He was also very good with the ball at his feet.'

Robin van Persie, a long-term champion of youth, was similarly impressed by his fledgling team-mate's display. 'Paddy did great,' he enthused. 'I know how hard it is to make your debut. I made mine in Holland for Feyenoord and he made his for Manchester United in front of seventy-five thousand people, at home, in a difficult period. He did really well on the ball. His decision-making was great and defensively he stood up well. It was great for him.'

A first-team debut was just the latest instalment in McNair's rapid ascent at United, the club he joined as a 14-year-old after learning his early craft at Ballyclare Colts in Northern Ireland. Having graduated from Ashton-on-Mersey School in Sale, he continued his education by converting into a ball-playing centre-back position, having previously played on the wing or as a deep-lying forward. 'I think I will mainly play in defence for the rest of my career, but I still think I can play in midfield,' he admitted. 'So it is a case of either/or. I don't mind as long as I'm playing.'

Incredibly, Paddy took his bow for the Under-21s only in February 2014, which prompted Reserves manager Warren Joyce to describe him as the 'most-improved' player to emerge from the Reds' factory line of talent over the previous 12 months. 'I thought he had a really good end to the 2013-14 season,' Joyce said. 'He was consistent and worked really hard on one-versus-one defending. His physical attributes kicked in from Christmas onwards and he is cool under pressure.'

Given the fact that van Gaal cherishes players who are adaptable, certainly in terms of positioning, McNair can rightfully look forward to more first-team opportunities in the coming months and years.

35. JESSE LINGARD

Position: Attacker
Born: 15 December 1992; Warrington, England
Previous clubs: Leicester City, Birmingham City, Brighton & Hove Albion (all loans)
Joined United: 1 July 2009

Debut: 16 August 2014 vs Swansea City (H), Premier League
Honours: None

A local lad with style, verve and a habit of entertaining supporters with fast, free-flowing football, Jesse Lingard is arguably the personification of a Manchester United Academy graduate. The attacking midfielder was born in Warrington, Cheshire – just 19 miles from Old Trafford – and has ascended through the ranks at the Aon Training Complex, developing under the tutelage of Paul McGuinness, Warren Joyce and, of course, former Reserve team manager Ole Gunnar Solskjaer.

Having won the prestigious FA Youth Cup in 2011 alongside midfield partners Paul Pogba and Ravel Morrison, Lingard made his first venture into the first team during the 2012 pre-season tour of South Africa, Shanghai and Europe, where a series of impressive cameos prompted Sir Alex Ferguson to later place him on the bench for League Cup ties with Newcastle United and Chelsea. Later that season, in November, the youngster agreed to join Leicester City on loan to obtain first-team experience in the rough and tumble of the Championship, a division tailor-made for transforming boys into men. After five invaluable outings for the Foxes, Jesse returned home to help his United team-mates win the inaugural Barclays Under-21 Premier League, finishing the season with seven goals and 26 appearances for Joyce's youngsters.

Another eye-catching pre-season tour under a new manager followed, this time under the guidance of David Moyes. Impressively, the youngster was United's top scorer on tour, netting five times, and he returned home with his burgeoning reputation enhanced. At this time, Reds legend Paul Scholes felt Lingard was a 'better prospect' than Adnan Januzaj, though it was the Belgian whose chance to shine arrived first. Meanwhile, Jesse was sent on loan to Birmingham City, for whom he scored four times on his debut before hitting two more in 16 appearances. 'It was an unbelievable start for Jesse,' commented Joyce. 'It was

Roy of the Rovers stuff; you could not write a script like that.'

Another temporary stay was ordered in March 2014, this time at Brighton & Hove Albion, where the 21-year-old helped the Seagulls reach the play-off final as an influential component of their attack. Although disappointed to miss out on the fairytale ending that was promotion to the top flight, Lingard was thankful for the experience and determined to press on at United. 'I learned so much from the loan spells last season,' Jesse said. 'Playing in front of big crowds every week was great for my confidence and I was starting every game too, against tough opposition. I think it will hopefully stand me in good stead.'

The 2014-15 campaign required Lingard to adapt to another new manager in the form of Louis van Gaal, a self-styled trainer-coach who is known for trusting in the courage and adaptability of young players. True to his philosophy, the Dutchman awarded Lingard his much-anticipated first-team debut as right wing-back during the opening-day defeat to Swansea City but, while a first-half knee injury cruelly cut short his moment in the spotlight, the Academy graduate has time on his side and should expect another crack at Old Trafford stardom. After all, he is a product of Manchester United, a club built on overcoming adversity.

36. MARNICK VERMIJL

Position: Defender
Born: 13 January 1992; Peer, Belgium
Previous clubs: Standard Liege, NEC Nijmegen (loan)
Joined United: 1 July 2010
Debut: 26 September 2012 vs Newcastle United (H), League Cup
Honours: None

Signed from Standard Liege before he had even made his senior debut for the Belgian side, Marnick Vermijl arrived in Manchester as a highly rated youngster and has not disappointed in his time with United.

A right-back by trade in his four years with the Reds, the Belgian youth international stands out for his versatility – unsurprisingly so, considering his nomadic positional journey. 'When I was young, I started out as a striker,' he revealed. 'But down the years I went a position back and then a position back. I was actually a central defender until I was sixteen or seventeen and then started to play right-back, even though I'd never played there before. You need to get forward from the right-back position. I think it's the most enjoyable part of football as well.'

It takes special levels of intelligence and fitness to be able to function in such a wide variety of positions, and Marnick boasts high quantities of both. A regular in the Reds' Under-21s, he is one of the most dependable performers the club has had during recent seasons, having quickly assimilated after his 2010 arrival at the Aon Training Complex. As a boyhood United fan, Marnick had idolised Gary Neville and the opportunity to join United in 2010 felt, in the Belgian's words, 'like a dream'.

Vermijl's impressive early displays in the youth ranks laid bare his eye-catching consistency, in much the same fashion that then-club captain Neville had made his name at the highest level. 'It's an important part of the game to be consistent as well as everything else,' said the Belgian. 'It's about working hard every day in training to make sure you have enough in your tank to get those games under your belt. You need to get your chance and then you need to perform.'

That opportunity at senior level came in the 2012 Capital One Cup victory over Newcastle United. Sir Alex Ferguson included Vermijl in a defence which contained four debutants, yet still managed to progress with a 2-1 victory – much to the Belgian's delight. 'I was a bit nervous before the game, but I think that's normal if you're going to play in such a big stadium for such a big team,' he admitted. 'I really enjoyed it – with all the young lads playing, and to get the win and go through, made it even better.'

Buoyed by the experience, Vermijl went on to complete an impressive remainder of the 2012-13 campaign in Warren Joyce's Under-21s, earning a spot on the three-man shortlist for the Denzil Haroun Reserve Team Player of the Year award. A regular collector of team silverware with Joyce's all-conquering second string, Marnick sampled sustained senior action in 2013-14 with a season-long loan to NEC Nijmegen in the Netherlands.

Though his temporary side were relegated from the Dutch top flight, his displays on the right side of their defence were consistently impressive. While he was disappointed to miss out on the 2014 pre-season tour of the United States, his form since returning to Old Trafford prompted Louis van Gaal to offer further first-team football in the Capital One Cup defeat to MK Dons.

37. SAIDY JANKO

Position: Defender
Born: 22 October 1995; Zurich, Switzerland
Previous clubs: FC Zurich
Joined United: 2 September 2013
Debut: 26 August 2014 vs MK Dons (A), League Cup
Honours: None

While it was Adnan Januzaj who took home the Player of the Tournament award at the 2013 Blue Stars tournament, United's travelling scouts had their attention taken by a local talent: the powerful Saidy Janko. As one of the stars of the FC Zurich team which won the prestigious competition, the quicksilver, right-sided defender impressed sufficiently to earn himself a trial with the Reds – although the interest came as a huge surprise to Saidy himself.

'A lot of people came up to me and said I'd played well, but I never expected something like that happening,' he conceded. 'I'd never heard anything about United being interested or impressed with me. Of course, I knew all about United because I followed the Premier League and everything around it – even if I confess I used to be an Arsenal fan!'

The athletic youngster performed well enough during his summer trial at the Aon Training Complex to earn a deadline-day move to the club, and thereafter caught the eye after slotting straight into Warren Joyce's Under-21s for the remainder of the 2013-14 term, as well as Nicky Butt's Under-19s for the Reds' brief but thrilling assault on the UEFA Youth League.

Having coached Janko alongside Butt, club legend Paul Scholes was in no doubt of the youngster's potential. 'Saidy has been fantastic since he came in and looks a bright prospect for the future,' said the former United and England midfielder. 'Hopefully he is on his way to the first team.'

Youth League duties dictated that Janko and his Under-19s colleagues travelled with David Moyes's first team to all three away games during the seniors' Champions League group campaign, and the Swiss starlet admitted: 'You always see them and think: "One day, I want to be up the front with the first team on the plane."'

In the short term, Saidy demonstrated that he was more than just talk, by maintaining fine form throughout his first season with the Reds, to the point that he was named the Denzil Haroun Reserve Team Player of the Year in recognition. 'I've settled in pretty well because Manchester United is like a family, so I made friends really quickly,' said the defender, whose immaculate English stems from his father's regular use of the language. 'That is why it wasn't that difficult to settle in when I came here,' he added. 'I spend time with the foreign boys and help them as well sometimes.'

Utilised as a right-back, midfielder and right-winger during his maiden campaign in Manchester, Janko made his first-team debut in a position which incorporated aspects of all his previous roles: wing-back. 'I don't mind where I play,' he said. 'I've played there before in

Switzerland for both FC Zurich and the international team as well.'

Though his bow came in the nightmarish Capital One Cup defeat at MK Dons, Saidy was far from overawed by the occasion, and he retains a burning desire to feature regularly for the senior side. 'I am pleased but I still feel hungry,' he said. 'The club has taught me so many things. When I think now about a year ago, I didn't even know football. Now I've learned quite a lot from people here. I know how big everything is and how big football can be. I wasn't used to that before. I still want more and that is good.'

39. TOM THORPE

Position: Defender
Born: 13 January 1993; Manchester, England
Previous clubs: Birmingham City (loan)
Joined United: 1 July 2009
Debut: 27 September 2014 vs West Ham United (H), Premier League
Honours: None

As a lifelong United fan whose father regularly took him to Old Trafford, it is fair to say that Tom Thorpe achieved a lifelong ambition when making his first-team debut during 2014's nail-biting victory over West Ham, as an injury-time replacement for club-record signing Angel Di Maria.

The tall, uncompromising centre-back was called upon by Louis van Gaal at the 11th hour as the Dutchman sought reinforcements in the absence of four regular defenders. Even though Northern Irish team-mate Paddy McNair was ultimately chosen to partner Marcos Rojo in the middle, Thorpe was able to draw great pride from his short-lived introduction to senior football.

Like all young players, his arrival on the biggest stage was the culmination of his own hard graft and determination, having worked his way through the club's illustrious youth system with one eye fixed firmly on the first team. 'I've been here since I was seven and going down to The Cliff and then Littleton Road,' Thorpe explained. 'I used to get brought to training sessions every night and visit Carrington every now and then. I live in Denton, which is only fifteen minutes or so away, and it's brilliant to be playing for the club you support.'

A natural leader with excellent communication skills, it was almost inevitable that Tom would wear the captain's armband for the youth ranks, and it was under his leadership that United claimed the 2011 FA Youth Cup with an eye-catching team that included the likes of Paul Pogba and the Keane twins, as well as West Ham prospect Ravel Morrison.

Thorpe has since cemented his place in Warren Joyce's team and built a reputation as a centre-back of great composure and skill. He was unlucky not to win the Denzil Haroun Reserve Team Player of the Year away in 2013 at the end of a season that followed a positive summer with the national team.

'I was captain of England when we went to the Under-19 European Championship in 2012,' Tom recalled. 'It was a good experience as well as a very proud moment for me. We got to the semi-finals, but we should have won against Greece. There were a few hitches here and there, but we should have reached the final. I'm always pleased to be captain, though, whether it is for the club or my country.'

Now that he has made a first-team debut for United, and having sampled a taste of the big time, the young Reds defender is hungry for another course and has drawn inspiration from other Academy graduates who have already cemented their place among the playing staff at Old Trafford.

'The evidence is there that if you work hard and do well then you get the chance,' he acknowledged. 'If you take that chance then you're on your way. It's been the history of Manchester United, with lads from young ages who have come through the Academy, pushed on into the first team and progressed from there. Hopefully, I can do the same as them.'

40. BEN AMOS

Position: Goalkeeper
Born: 10 April 1990; Macclesfield, England
Previous clubs: Peterborough United, FK Molde, Oldham Athletic, Hull City, Carlisle United (all loans)
Joined United: 1 July 2006
Debut: 23 September 2008 vs Middlesbrough (H), League Cup
Honours: FIFA Club World Cup (2008)

The trouble with being a goalkeeper is that there is only one position in the team, and when your main competition is David De Gea, life isn't easy. However, Ben Amos boasts an impressive determination that will underpin a fine professional career in football.

The Macclesfield-born stopper arrived at United as an 11-year-old and has steadily climbed the ranks ever since, joining the Academy at 16 before making his first-team debut just two years later in a routine League Cup third-round victory over Middlesbrough. Having convinced United's coaching staff of his potential, he was picked as a late replacement for the injured Ben Foster as Sir Alex Ferguson's European champions travelled to Japan to win the Club World Cup.

Like most youngsters, Amos spent much of his early career on the road and gained experience via separate loan spells with Peterborough (2009), Molde (2010) and Oldham Athletic (2011). A Premier League debut against Stoke City followed, before a new three-year deal was inked in May 2012, underlining the club's belief in his abilities. Another temporary stay was just around the corner, however, this time with Hull City at the outset of the 2012-13 season.

Nineteen appearances later, Ben felt ready to challenge for a place at Old Trafford under new manager, David Moyes.

Unfortunately, with results going sour on the pitch, the under-fire Scot could not afford to rest De Gea and Amos was denied his opportunity to shine. 'Last season was a bit of a non-season for me, to be honest,' Ben explained at the end of the campaign. 'I waited to go on loan early doors, as I fancied having a go at impressing the manager. As it turned out, I didn't get an opportunity so that left me looking for games. I went on loan to Carlisle, got those minutes under my belt and really enjoyed that.'

Now in the year of his 25th birthday, Amos knows he must impress and hopes to quickly earn the trust of Louis van Gaal and new goalkeeping coach Frans Hoek, the renowned trainer who is best known for his work with Edwin van der Sar at Ajax. After soaking up the knowledge of former mentors Eric Steele and Chris Woods, Ben remains keen to enhance his education: 'We've had three goalkeeper coaches now in three years, but I don't think that's a bad thing,' he said. 'It's a different angle, a different opinion, a different philosophy on the game. That can really help you if you cherry-pick the best bits from all those coaches. I think it can only benefit me in the long run.'

Looking forward, United's home-grown keeper remains focused on the plan and refuses to extinguish the fire that burns inside of him. 'Hopefully I can force my way in and get some games,' he says. 'Everybody starts on the same page and everyone's out to impress the new manager. All being well, I can make a positive impression.'

41. REECE JAMES

Position: Defender

Born: 7 November 1993; Bacup, England

Previous clubs: Blackburn Rovers, Preston North End (both youth), Carlisle United (loan)

Joined United: 1 July 2012
Debut: 26 August 2014 vs MK Dons (A), League Cup
Honours: None

In the baking heat of the Rose Bowl in Pasadena, California, where United held a 3-0 lead in a pre-season encounter with LA Galaxy, Reece James, an unexpected member of Louis van Gaal's 23-man touring squad, limbered up ahead of his first-ever senior appearance for the Reds. The youngster had had 24 hours to prepare mentally, but at no point in that time could he have foreseen how his debut would unfold.

At the sound of the final whistle, the 20-year-old Lancashire lad walked off the pitch with two goals to his name from a comprehensive 7-0 victory over the team made by famous by David Beckham's American adventure. His first was a lovely left-footed finish past goalkeeper Jaime Penedo from 12 yards, his second an instinctive rebound effort from the edge of the area. It was 4am back home in Bacup, where a hefty group of Reece's family had gathered to watch the game on television, and the congregation watched on in disbelief. It barely seemed credible to the player, either.

'I hadn't scored for United at any level, so the first goal was a special moment,' he explained. 'I was in a bit of shock. I just turned and looked for the first player who was running towards me. And when the second one went in, I couldn't believe it was actually happening – it was just my lucky day. At full time I had a look around to take it all in, and then the first thing I thought about was what my mum and dad would have been doing. I phoned home as soon as I got on the coach and my dad couldn't believe it. Both of my parents were quite emotional but they were really proud.'

For James, this was the culmination of his hard work since earning a full-time contract in July 2012, just two months after his older brother Matty had left the club to join Leicester City. His solid form in 2012-13 helped Warren Joyce's second string win the inaugural

Barclays Under-21 Premier League, before he earned one of three nominations for the club's Young Player of the Year award – which eventually went to Swiss powerhouse Saidy Janko.

Having since impressed on this summer's pre-season tour of America, not just against Galaxy but also during a 3-2 win over AS Roma, the youngster's real reward was a place on the bench for the opening-day match with Swansea City. A competitive debut during the Capital One Cup trip to MK Dons also followed, ensuring his place in history as a senior United player. Having sampled a taste of the first-team experience, James is hungry for more.

'When I go down for food and see some of the faces around the room, like Rooney and Mata, it hits me that you don't do things like this in everyday life,' James conceded. 'I want to get used to it and I hope I can be a part of it for a lot longer.'

42. TYLER BLACKETT

Position: Defender
Born: 2 April 1994; Manchester, England
Previous clubs: Blackpool, Birmingham City (both loans)
Joined United: 1 July 2012
Debut: 16 August 2014 vs Swansea City (H), Premier League
Honours: None

Louis van Gaal arrived at Manchester United with a reputation for trusting young, adaptable players whom he could mould to fit his own philosophy. It was built over the course of a long and successful managerial career, but the foundation was undoubtedly laid by his Ajax side that lifted the 1995 Champions League trophy with an average age of just 23. Indeed, were it not for the two veterans, Danny Blind and Frank Rijkaard, the Dutch giants could easily have been mistaken for a youth team.

Upon van Gaal's appointment at Old Trafford, United fans speculated over which Academy starlet would benefit most and while Blackett was certainly in contention, it is fair to say the Manchester-born defender was not among the frontrunners. However, Blackett soon caught the manager's eye with a handful of strikingly assured pre-season performances and, as such, was named in the starting XI for the opening-day clash with Swansea City at Old Trafford, where his first-team debut was witnessed by 75,339 fans. It was a considerable step up, considering he had spent the preceding campaign on loan at Championship clubs Blackpool and Birmingham City, playing for experience and in front of crowds of around 10,000 spectators.

The youngster continued to shine following his first-team bow, registering a number of Premier League starts that enhanced this precocious talent's burgeoning reputation. 'Pre-season went well for me, I concentrated on what I needed to do and I've had a good start to the season as well,' he explained in September 2014. 'As a centre-back, training and working with these players is a part of my career that I've just got to look forward to and do my best. The manager told us all, right from the word go really, that he's not scared of using the young players, so we're all ready to go and try to prove that we can play at this level. It's been good for all of us.'

A local boy grounded in the ways of United, Blackett has been with the club since the age of eight and has steadily graduated through the Reds' ranks to become the 20-year-old prospect of today. With great height and an increasingly powerful physique, he is naturally suited to the centre-back position but has the technical abilities required to play on the left of defence or midfield, roles he has previously fulfilled at the request of Paul McGuiness and Warren Joyce further down the ranks.

Such versatility renders Blackett a valuable asset for van Gaal, who is on record for valuing 'team players' who can operate in various formations. Despite the arrivals of Argentinian defender Marcos Rojo and the versatile Daley Blind, son of the aforementioned Danny, the

Dutchman will know he possesses a rough diamond who could go on to play a considerable role in his Old Trafford revolution.

44. ANDREAS PEREIRA

Position: Midfielder
Born: 1 January 1996; Duffel, Belgium
Previous club: PSV Eindhoven (youth)
Joined United: 1 July 2012
United debut: 26 August 2014 vs MK Dons (A), League Cup
Honours: None

Another United youngster to make his debut in the forgettable Capital One Cup mauling at MK Dons in August 2014, Andreas Pereira's reputation remains untainted by such a shocking introduction to senior football. The Belgium-born schemer arrived at the Aon Training Complex from PSV Eindhoven in 2012 with huge expectations, and nothing he displayed in his first two seasons at United did anything to alter that. Nicky Butt, who coached the teenager, is in no doubt of his potential.

'Andreas is a tricky player,' said the former Reds midfielder. 'He's Andres Iniesta-like coming off the left onto his right foot and can play from the right, too. He's very young, still maturing, he needs to be aware it is not all about trickery and sometimes you have to show how good you are doing the simple things – then every now and then show a bit of magic. If he learns that he can be a superstar; he's got the X-factor you need to play at this club.'

That penchant for the biggest stage has always been in Andreas's game, allowing him to stand out when it matters most. Scouted after stealing the show at the 2012 Nike Premier Cup tournament at the Aon Training Complex, he also shone in the Reds' successful Milk Cup campaign of 2013 and can already boast of goals on

219

his first outings at Old Trafford and Anfield in his fledgling career.

Patience is a virtue for any young player aiming to rise through the ultra-competitive ranks at United, but Pereira has already demonstrated his willingness to play the waiting game, as he was restricted to nothing more than training in his opening months with the club while his paperwork was processed. 'I had to wait three or four months for my clearance,' he recalled. 'I was actually training when they said I could play, so I went on the bus to Sheffield [for an Under-18s game against Sheffield Wednesday]. When we got there, it was raining so hard that, after about half an hour, they had to stop the game!'

When Andreas – whose brother Joel is also on the club's books, as a goalkeeper – did finally get a sustained run of competitive action, he announced himself as a talented attacking midfielder with an eye for the spectacular. A dead-ball specialist, either going for goal or supplying ammunition for his colleagues, he puts in extra work on his set-pieces every day in training, and he acknowledges that practice is the best route to improvement.

'You have to change the way you train and work harder every day,' he said. 'I feel you must try to develop every single day if you want to get into the first team, and I realise you have to work very hard. I think a lot of people believe being a footballer is easy – if you can kick a ball, it's okay. But it is very hard work – not only on the pitch but off the pitch as well. If you go home, you have to make sure you rest and other things like that.'

Having seen fellow Belgium-born youngster Adnan Januzaj progress from United's youth set-up to first team regularity, Andreas admits: 'It's a motivation to see him doing well and doing everything right because you know what you have to do.'

The impressive self-confidence and aptitude on show in Pereira's first-team debut – despite the scoreline – suggest that he has learned from the lessons of his close friend, and has the ability to spend more time with him at senior level.

48. WILL KEANE

Position: Striker
Born: 11 January 1993; Stockport, England
Previous clubs: Wigan Athletic, Queens Park Rangers (both loans)
Joined United: 1 July 2009
Debut: 31 December 2011 vs Blackburn Rovers (H), Premier League
Honours: None

Will Keane is one of the most potent and technically gifted strikers to emerge from the club's Academy in recent history – despite suffering a career-threatening injury that cruelly curtailed his development at the end of his most prolific season at United.

Having made his first-team debut on the final day of 2011, coming on as a substitute during a shock Premier League home defeat to Blackburn Rovers, the Stockport lad was on the brink of stardom. He had even been promised a place in the senior squad by Sir Alex Ferguson, with Dimitar Berbatov edging closer to the exit door following his omission from the manager's Champions League final squad.

However, football can be a cruel game and at the end of an impressive campaign that yielded 19 goals for the Reserves, the 19-year-old twin brother of Reds defender Mike Keane ruptured cruciate knee ligaments while representing England's Under-19s against Switzerland. Over 16 months of rehabilitation ensued, with plenty of hours spent in the gym with physio Richard Merron, until Keane was finally ready to make his return to action in November 2013. Understandably, those around him were suitably determined to restore his immeasurable abilities.

'I don't think there was a better player at his age in the country at the time he got injured,' opined Warren Joyce, when quizzed on the former Jimmy Murphy Player of the Year and FA Youth Cup winner. 'So we're mindful that the most important thing is getting him back to that level. Then he's got to kick on again to see how close he can get to the first team.'

Having made a successful comeback during the second half of the 2013-14 season, a period that involved separate loan spells at Wigan Athletic and Queens Park Rangers, Keane is eager to make up for lost time and has drawn inspiration from Roy Keane and Alan Shearer, two players who both overcame similar knee problems during their illustrious careers. 'Once you've had a serious injury, you look into it a lot more and realise many of the top-class players have had setbacks, come through it and managed to return to the same level,' he said.

Looking forward, Keane has a fight on his hands with Wayne Rooney, Robin van Persie, Radamel Falcao and fellow Academy graduate James Wilson all duking it out for first-team places up front. But with a new manager at the helm, United's comeback kid is confident of catching the eye and hopes to take giant strides in the near future.

'Once a new manager comes in, it's a fresh start for everyone,' Will said. 'The manager has a great track record and has said players' experience is not just based on age; it's about taking responsibility whether you're young or old. If you're doing the job he wants you to do, he gives you the confidence that you'll get an opportunity. That's what I want to do.'

49. JAMES WILSON

Position: Striker
Born: 1 December 1995; Biddulph, England
Previous clubs: None
Joined United: 1 July 2012
United debut: 6 May 2014 vs Hull City (H), Premier League
Honours: None

'It was a great feeling; you can't compare it to anything else,' grinned 18-year-old James Wilson, having marked his Premier League debut with two of United's goals in a 3-1 victory over Hull City at Old Trafford. Only the 13th player in the club's history to have scored more than once on his debut, the England youth international went on: 'The first goal was just sheer euphoria and then the second was just a great experience. The ground is a lot different without 75,000 people, but just to play here even in front of a small crowd for the Under-21s is still a great experience to play on such a ground. With all the fans here tonight it was even better.

'I feel like I can deal with the physicality and pace of the game. I just need to try to get as many games as possible under my belt for the experience. If you're getting on in the club, you have to be progressing, so obviously scoring for every age group is a good sign. I've got where I am now but I have to kick on.'

There is little doubt that Wilson has what it takes to do just that. While the 2014 sale of Danny Welbeck to Arsenal raised many eyebrows around football, reports suggested that the Longsight striker's departure was prompted by the news that his 18-year-old colleague was viewed by manager Louis van Gaal as a better prospect. The Dutchman's assistant, Ryan Giggs, gave Wilson his debut during his four-game stint as interim manager, and is well aware of the potential he contains.

'He's a goalscorer – a natural goalscorer; but he's got more to his game than just that,' said the Welshman. 'He can turn and run and he's a very clever player. I was delighted for him that he got two goals. If you give young players a chance, they will take it. I was proud to see that.'

Giggs's decision to blood Wilson against Steve Bruce's side was aided by a glowing recommendation from coach Nicky Butt, who had worked with the striker throughout his previous two seasons. 'Wilson is unbelievable in the six-yard box,' enthused Butt. 'He's got the best standing spring you've ever seen in your life.'

That unforgettable night, watched by his parents at Old Trafford, completed a staggering season's work for the teenager, who had represented the Under-18s, Under-19s, Under-21s and the senior side all in the same season. 'I'm definitely pleased,' he admitted. 'I've got through the three age groups and, as a striker, I want to score goals. I've done that at each level, but the most important thing is to keep improving – as long as that keeps happening. To get to where I am now, I have obviously improved.'

And how. Yet while Wilson was an overnight sensation in the eyes of many, his debut was the culmination of two-thirds of his life spent involved with the Reds. Having first come to the club's attention at the age of six, he steadily ascended the youth ranks and consistently excelled. His first outing at Old Trafford came while he was still a schoolboy, for Paul McGuinness's Under-18s in an FA Youth Cup quarter-final against Charlton Athletic, yet Wilson settled a thrilling game by rolling home a 97th-minute winner.

'I can remember being in the changing rooms afterwards and I was in the shower,' he reflected. 'It was boiling hot and everyone was touching the water and asking how I could bear to stand in it. It must have been because of the adrenaline! It was just a great feeling, particularly with it being the winner as well.'

A prolific figure in the Under-18s, Wilson has a remarkably professional approach for one so young, spouting mature maxims like: 'If I get a knock, I must get back up and go again' and 'Even in training, if you miss a chance, it matters.' It was unsurprising, then, he was entrusted with captaining both McGuinness's side and the Under-19s in their UEFA Youth League campaign of 2013-14. 'When I was told I'd be captain, I thought it was a great honour,' he confessed. 'Being given that responsibility meant I was able to give advice and encouragement on the pitch. It made me work harder, essentially, because when you have got the armband on, you have that extra responsibility to shine.'

And shine he did. Wilson's searing pace, football intelligence and ability to run with the ball unavoidably evoke memories of illustrious forebears, including current team-mate Robin van Persie. Patience must always be exercised when dealing with such fledgling talents, however, as Under-21s manager Warren Joyce stresses.

'James is still growing and his body is still developing,' explained Joyce. 'His fitness levels have improved greatly this season from last year, but he is still a developing boy. He's got a lot of potential and has that knack of scoring goals, but he needs to keep working hard. I have got to say that he is a grounded kid, but he must work harder now he's had a little bit of success.'

A thrilling debut at Old Trafford heightened expectations and, although injury disappointingly denied Wilson the chance to give van Gaal a sustained show of his capabilities in the 2014 pre-season campaign, he remained undeterred. Named in the Reserves' Manchester Senior Cup final side to face Manchester City, the teenager scored four goals in the space of 37 minutes to secure a thumping 4-1 victory for Joyce's side.

'He's got a lot of things he has still got to work on,' insisted Joyce. 'There are things, technically and tactically, he's naive on. He is still a young boy with a lot of natural talent. There are a lot of things he can still improve on, but he wants to do that and he can do it this year.' Wilson was equally even-handed about his staggering exploits, simply saying: 'Hopefully I can get the call-up to do it for the new gaffer [van Gaal] as well.'

Sure enough, the call soon came and Wilson was introduced as a substitute in the Reds' Capital One Cup trip to MK Dons. Coming close with two efforts which forced fine saves from Dons goalkeeper David Martin, the striker was the only United player to really catch the eye on an otherwise forgettable evening.

It is especially rare for a striker to rise through the United youth system and establish himself as a first-team fixture – Welbeck was the closest any had come since Mark Hughes in the late 1980s – but armed with a level head, devastating pace and an innate knack for scoring, Wilson has the potential to do just that.

50. SAM JOHNSTONE

Position: Goalkeeper
Born: 25 March 1993; Preston, England
Previous clubs: Oldham Athletic, Scunthorpe United, Walsall, Yeovil Town, Doncaster Rovers (all loans)
Joined United: 1 July 2009
United debut: TBC
Honours: None

Back in 2011, the replacement of Edwin van der Sar with David De Gea completely altered the dynamic of the goalkeeping ranks at United. Whereas previously, rank had run parallel to age, the club suddenly had three of its four senior squad stoppers aged between 19 and 21. For Sam Johnstone, the youngest of the quartet, De Gea's arrival in a roster also comprising Anders Lindegaard and Ben Amos allowed a tight bond to form between players who are ostensibly rivals.

'I think the four of us are close because we're similar ages,' he conceded. 'Obviously, when Edwin was here, everyone still got on with him but he was a bit older and wasn't into the same joking about that we were. We mess about because we're so close in age. We share the same interests and go out socially – playing snooker, shopping or eating out. Yet it's still competitive in training.'

As the youngest senior goalkeeper at the club, the physically imposing Johnstone knows that patience is one of the most important attributes he can possess. 'You just need someone to put their trust in you and then it's up to you to take the opportunity,' he said. 'Anything can happen. So it's a case of having patience but realising it can happen within the click of your fingers. You could be on the bench and even end up starting the game rather than coming on as the goalkeepers have an intense warm-up. If an injury does happen, then you're straight in.'

An injury to Lindegaard and Amos's absence on loan allowed Johnstone the experience of being an unused substitute during the 2012-13 campaign, including the Reds' unforgettable last-minute victory at reigning champions Manchester City in December 2012. 'I think the biggest experience for me was the derby,' he said. 'That was really good – a great game – and I was able to celebrate from the bench!'

Preston-born Johnstone has regularly featured for England at youth level, most notably winning UEFA's European Under-17s Championships in 2010, while highlights with the Reds so far have been winning the 2011 FA Youth Cup and saving three of four penalties in the 2012 National Reserves Play-off success against Aston Villa. Arguably more valuable, however, was a loan stint spent battling relegation with League One's Scunthorpe United.

'It helped me a lot,' he admitted. 'It was a difficult time when I was there, as they were fighting relegation and hovering around the drop-zone. It was a good team but they just couldn't get the results. It helped me to grow up from a little boy and into a man, so it was all about maturing. You have to do everything for yourself.'

That willingness to take responsibility, plus patience and his unquestionable pedigree, will be key in Johnstone's ongoing battle to emerge victorious in the friendly but fierce battle to become United's first-choice goalkeeper.

A Word from the Manager

It gave me a huge sense of pride to be asked to be the manager of Manchester United, and I have very much enjoyed my early months in the job. The fans of this wonderful football club are incredible – they gave me goosebumps when I first walked out as the manager at Old Trafford, and every time I have contact with them around Manchester they always make me feel very welcome in their city. I saw during our pre-season tour in the United States how big this football club really is. I knew it was enormous, of course, but the fanbase really is just incredible to witness as the manager.

I am delighted to test myself in English football. I have admired the Premier League for a number of years; it is a very hard league to win because it is very fast and very physical, but I am relishing the challenge of being here for the 2014-15 season and beyond. Of course, as I have said many times already at my press conferences, as a team we are now in a process which will take time.

Ed Woodward and the Glazer family hired me because of my philosophy as a coach, and to build up a new team at Manchester United. I bring another approach to the club and that is difficult because I have to provide the players with a lot of information, but

I am not a short-term coach. I am always thinking for the long term. You have to take measures that are not good for the short term, but it is better for the long term of the club. That may not be good for me as a coach, but I am not here for me as a coach, I am here for the club.

My coaching staff are very important to this process, and we are working very closely together. My assistant, Ryan Giggs, has played in the Premier League longer than any other player and I will draw upon that experience over the course of the season, while the rest of the coaching team each have their own strengths in their respective field of expertise. I am very happy with the backroom team I have assembled and the players will benefit from working with coaches who have such extensive knowledge.

It is important that we train and educate the players to perform as a team and not as individuals. I always train in the brains and not in the legs. The most important thing they have to know is why we do things. They have to think and know why they have to do certain things, rather than just doing it intuitively. This takes time, and so does the adaptation of the new players we have signed since I arrived. We now have a lot of creative players and it is another process to integrate these players and make them work within the team going forward, but also in a defensive way. This does not happen overnight, but all the time we are improving and I hope you are all excited for what the future holds. I certainly am.

Louis van Gaal

Fixture List Season 2014-15

Manchester United Season Guide 2014-15

Date	Fixture	H/A	KO	Competition
Sat 16 Aug	**Swansea City**	**H**	**12.45pm**	**Premier League**
Sun 24 Aug	Sunderland	A	4.00pm	Premier League
Wed 27 Aug	MK Dons	A	8.00pm	Capital One Cup 2
Sat 30 Aug	Burnley	A	12.45pm	Premier League
1-9 Sep				International Dates
Sun 14 Sep	**Queens Park Rangers**	**H**	**4.00pm**	**Premier League**
Sun 21 Sep	Leicester City	A	1.30pm	Premier League
Sat 27 Sep	**West Ham United**	**H**	**3.00pm**	**Premier League**
Sun 5 Oct	**Everton**	**H**	**12noon**	**Premier League**
6-14 Oct				International Dates
Mon 20 Oct	West Bromwich Albion	A	8.00pm	Premier League
Sun 26 Oct	**Chelsea**	**H**	**4.00pm**	**Premier League**
Sun 2 Nov	Manchester City	A	1.30pm	Premier League
Sat 8 Nov	**Crystal Palace**	**H**	**3.00pm**	**Premier League**
10-18 Nov				International Dates
Sat 22 Nov	Arsenal	A	5.30pm	Premier League
Sat 29 Nov	**Hull City**	**H**	**3.00pm**	**Premier League**
Tue 2 Dec	**Stoke City**	**H**	**8.00pm**	**Premier League**
Mon 8 Dec	Southampton	A	8.00pm	Premier League
Sun 14 Dec	**Liverpool**	**H**	**1.30pm**	**Premier League**
Sat 20 Dec	Aston Villa	A	3.00pm	Premier League
Fri 26 Dec	**Newcastle United**	**H**	**3.00pm**	**Premier League**
Sun 28 Dec	Tottenham Hotspur	A	12noon	Premier League
Thu 1 Jan	Stoke City	A	12:45pm	Premier League
Sat 3 Jan				FA Cup 3

Manchester United Football Club Fixtures Season 2014-15

Date	Fixture	H/A	KO	Competition
Sat 10 Jan	**Southampton**	H	3.00pm	**Premier League**
Sat 17 Jan	Queens Park Rangers	A	3.00pm	Premier League
Sat 24 Jan				FA Cup 4
Sat 31 Jan	**Leicester City**	H	3.00pm	**Premier League**
Sat 7 Feb	West Ham United	A	3.00pm	Premier League
Tue 10 Feb	**Burnley**	H	8.00pm	**Premier League**
Sat 14 Feb				FA Cup 5
Sat 21 Feb	Swansea City	A	3.00pm	Premier League
Sat 28 Feb	**Sunderland**	H	3.00pm	**Premier League**
Wed 4 Mar	Newcastle United	A	7.45pm	Premier League
Sat 7 Mar				FA Cup 6
Sat 14 Mar	**Tottenham Hotspur**	H	3.00pm	**Premier League**
Sat 21 Mar	Liverpool	A	3.00pm	Premier League
23-31 Mar				International Dates
Sat 4 Apr	**Aston Villa**	H	3.00pm	**Premier League**
Sat 11 Apr	**Manchester City**	H	3.00pm	**Premier League**
Sat 18 Apr	Chelsea	A	3.00pm	Premier League
				FA Cup Semi Final
Sat 25 Apr	Everton	A	3.00pm	Premier League
Sat 2 May	**West Bromwich Albion**	H	3.00pm	**Premier League**
Sat 9 May	Crystal Palace	A	3.00pm	Premier League
Sat 16 May	**Arsenal**	H	3.00pm	**Premier League**
Sun 24 May	Hull City	A	3.00pm	Premier League
Sat 30 May				FA Cup Final

All kick-off times shown are UK time
All fixtures and kick-off times are subject to change

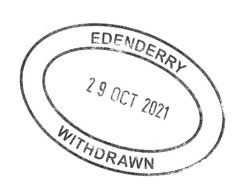